# Texas

# Hysterical

# Society

## The Wacky Side
## of the Lone Star State

## James E. Gaskin

Head Honcho, Texas Hysterical Society
with the support of the THS Honchos and Honchettes

ISBN
1-933177-37-3 (10 digit)
978-1-933177-37-3 (13 digit)

Library of Congress Control Number: 2011910854

First Edition

Line Art by David Gaskin, second cousin to the author

Printed in the United States of America
Published by WAGbooks, LLC
www.WAGbooks.com

As always, this and everything else is for
Wendy, Alex, and Laura

# Table of Contents

# Introduction

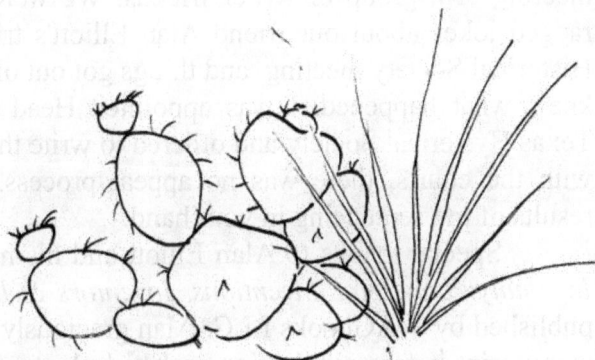

Real historians too often present history as a series of facts and events, but it's really about people. And people, especially Texans, can be wacky at times. And those of us with no professional historian credentials to protect can add the wacky stuff that too often gets forgotten back into history.

If you're not familiar with the Texas Hysterical Society, don't feel bad. We're small, new, a bit wacky ourselves, and don't pretend to be an official group of great import. And as funny as life in Texas is on a regular basis, we believe people should laugh more, embrace life, and be as Texan as possible every day of the year.

Texas history isn't all that old, but it is certainly rich and full. We can only report a small number of the stories that illustrate the wackiness that is Texas.

More interesting people arrive every day, and their actions tell us many hope to be named an Honorary Texan soon. If you can't be born Texan, being appointed an Honorary Texan by the Texas Hysterical Society is the next best thing. Well, it's better than a rash. Those striving to be named Honorary Texans should contact us for the requirements. We can be bribed.

The Texas Hysterical Society started during a lunch meeting of a group of writer friends. We were making some ragged jokes about our friend Alan Elliott's trip to the Texas Historical Society meeting, and things got out of hand. Before I knew what happened, I was appointed Head Honcho of the Texas Hysterical Society and ordered to write this book. Unlike with the courts, there was no appeal process. You hold the results of my sentencing in your hand.

Special thanks to Alan Elliott and his new book *Texas Ingenuity: Lone Star Inventions, Inventors & Innovators*, also published by WAGbooks LLC. Alan graciously let me read the manuscript before publication so I had plenty of time to steal, um, research the stories in his book. Unlike my book, his book is filled with well-researched facts and information. However, my book has more Aggie jokes.

In spite of our less than serious tone, the facts in the book are accurate. When you can't tell the facts from the jokes, you're in Texas.

The cover photo, taken by the outstanding (and wacky) Mark Davis (DavisStudios.com), shows the Texas Hysterical Society judges: me, Biz Haddock, and Alan Elliott. After a fierce battle throwing rock-paper-scissors, Biz got to wear the dress. Lucky Biz (and lucky readers).

I already mentioned Alan's new book *Texas Ingenuity* (TexasIngenuity.com), so let me praise Biz's singing group, Lantana. Three girls with hot... harmonies (LantanaMusic.com).

Line art in the book is from my second cousin, David Gaskin. Thanks, cuz.

Go to TexasHystericalSociety.com for a regular dose of new and old Texas stories with our special viewpoint. There are no dues for membership in the Texas Hysterical Society, but donations of money, or stories new and old, are gratefully accepted.

James E. Gaskin
Mesquite, TX
July, 2011

# Hysterical
# Historical
# Texas

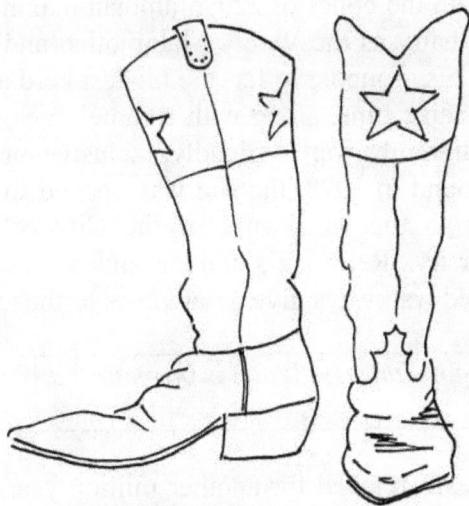

## *Texas Way Back When*

In the beginning... wait, that's another book, and we don't need to rehash the "God made Texas on the 8th day" jokes. But before the Bible, before people, before even the dinosaurs, there was Texas.

It was underwater for millions of years, of course, a trend that repeats with disastrous consequences for Galveston Island every 100 years or so. Modern Texas is still close to the water, with about 370 miles of coastline on the Gulf of Mexico and over 1,000 miles of channels, all, it seems, filled with oil tankers around Houston.

Want to jump in your WayBack Machine and see evidence of really old Texas? Head to Glen Rose, a bit southwest of Fort Worth at the north edge of the Texas Hill Country. Walk the same ground as dinosaurs did 110 million years ago at the Dinosaur Valley State Park. Play paleontologist in the 150-acre park and follow the dinosaur footprints. Go to Dinosaur World next door and look at 100 life size dinosaur models.

When you're tired of dinosaurs, try the Waco Mammoth Site with the bones of 22 Columbian mammoths, related to but not as hairy as the Wooly Mammoths (and Woolies got better PR). This group is, so far, the biggest herd ever found that died at the same time, along with a camel. Yes, a camel. Evidently the mammoths were a friendly, inclusive bunch.

Found in 1978, the site was opened to the public in 2009 thanks to the hard work of the City of Waco and Baylor University. Relax, it's indoor and air conditioned, and the elevated walkways give great views of the mammoths.

> *Hint for Yankees: Waco is pronounced Way-ko, not Wacko.*
> *— The Old Cowboy*

Texas relaxed for another million years or so, waiting for early people to make it across the Bering Strait from Russia and wander down to Texas. Next time someone says illegal immigration is a new problem, remember those poor Russian wanderers were here first.

Illegal immigration really kicked into gear when that crazy Christopher Columbus finally discovered America, or at least some islands close by. The protestations of those with Nordic ancestry are hereby noted by the Texas Hysterical Society, but we wish to remind them that their ancestors discovered Newfoundland, not Texas, so they don't really count either. That said, you get points for beating Columbus to the new world by about 500 years, but lose points for not sending waves of "explorers" looking to plunder the new found territory.

## *Europeans Arrive*
The first European group to see Texas was led by Spaniard Alonso Alverez de Pineda mapping the coastline from Florida to Vera Cruz in 1519. Whether you consider this the bringing of civilization to the New World or the rape of an indigenous culture by European profiteers matters not to the Texas Hysterical Society at this point. Argue amongst yourselves.

> *You know, sometimes when you study history, you're stuck in the past.*
> — *George W. Bush, Honorary Texan*

The earliest tourist through inland Texas was Cabeza de Vaca starting in 1527. He was with another Spanish group sailing to Florida from Cuba planning to colonize and conquer the newfound Gulf Coast area. Cabeza and his group wandered around Florida but missed the boat back to Cuba, stranding them in this new place. And you thought missing an airplane was tough – how about being abandoned by your shipmates and stranded in a foreign wilderness?

Rag tag rafts were the order of the day, and the near-starving group finally hit land in November 1528, on Galveston Island. Indians found them, and Cabeza, smarter or perhaps less dead than the rest of his group, gave the Indian warriors some trinkets. Ah, trinkets, the universal persuader of American Indians (see the Manhattan Hysterical Society for their trinket story).

The trinkets, as always, worked, and the Indian warriors returned with food rather than more warriors and weapons. Well, maybe the trinkets didn't work as well in Texas as in Manhattan, because our buddy Cabeza and his few remaining friends were held captive for about six years before escaping. He wandered for two years across Texas heading westward until he found a Spanish outpost on the Gulf of California in May of 1536.

Unfortunately, Cabeza de Vaca couldn't keep his mouth shut and wrote about the beauty of Texas, embellishing the tales with some color (he called Galveston Island Malhado, or Island of Doom). His hyperbole convinced wannabe conquerors to come looking for riches like the fabulously wealthy Seven Cities of Cibola and the Golden Land of Quivira.

Francisco Vásquez de Coronado led over 1400 Spaniards and Indians to search for these great treasures. Luckily, Coronado found not the golden city of Quivira but central Kansas. Oops. His failure to hit the jackpot discouraged other explorers, and few Spaniards settled in Texas. But they do get the honor of being the first flag to fly over Texas, probably because the Indians only had a loincloth tied to a stick. Doesn't count.

The French arrived in 1685, starting a settlement in Matagordo Bay, Texas. That nearly 150 year stretch is the longest time between tourist seasons ever for Texas. Led by René Robert Cavelier, Sieur de La Salle (that's a long name for a business card), the colony didn't do well. Killed by his own men in 1687, La Salle's fort was attacked and destroyed by Indians two years later. Guess the French forgot their trinkets.

Spanish folks, even though they didn't seem to want Texas, didn't want the French to move westward from Louisiana and take it. We give the French credit for the second flag over Texas, although France gave their Louisiana territory to Spain in 1762. Why? The French didn't want Great Britain to take over the area after defeating the French in a European war. Insert your own "French can't fight" joke here.

New Spain had trouble keeping their borders safe, and the Mississippi River is a lot harder to swim across than the Rio Grande. Anglos started sneaking across the borders and wandering around exploring, and probably taking jobs away from the local residents and increasing Welfare rolls. The New Spain authorities kept locking them up, but immigrants kept appearing.

> *George Washington was really born in Texas.*
> *After he chopped down the mesquite tree, he told his father,*
> *"I cannot tell a lie." His father immediately started packing*
> *to move to Virginia.*
> *"But why, Father, did I disgrace the family?"*
> *"No, son, because if you can't tell a lie, you'll never*
> *succeed in Texas."*

Mexico rebelled against Spain in 1810, and finally won their independence in 1821. One of the immigrants they jailed for years, Peter Ellis Bean from Tennessee, helped Mexico win their battle to separate from Spain. Hmm, if only the story of an immigrant helping his adopted country had some relevance to our modern immigration issues.

Little details like France taking back Louisiana, then selling it to the United States in 1803, didn't stop the Mexican flag, Number Three, from flying over Texas from 1821 until 1836.

Unfriendly Indians kept Mexico from colonizing Texas the way they wanted, because Mexican citizens refused to move to Texas. Indian raids were common and fierce, and few colonists rushed into the new area, despite great deals on prime real estate. Too bad the Mexican government didn't read Spanish history and discover the magic powers trinkets had over unfriendly Indians.

Anglos, either braver or stupider than Mexican citizens (or equipped with trinkets), were happy to settle in Texas. The fact the Mexican government didn't really want them there made Texas all the sweeter.

## Texas Revolts

Stephen F. Austin convinced the Mexican government to allow him to bring in 300 families. In return, Austin promised to force the colonists to follow Mexican ideals and values, including becoming Catholics. And you thought tithing was tough.

More Anglos came streaming in (they get here, they send money to their relatives, and soon the whole family is sneaking across the border). In 1834, Mexicans in the area only numbered about 7,800, while Anglo immigrants were up to about 30,000.

Mexico did what governments almost always do: the wrong thing. The new Mexican dictator, Antonio Lóde Santa Anna, raised taxes and generally tried to make things miserable for the Texans with extra rules and restrictions. He declared the border closed to new immigrants in 1830. He'd already crushed several uprisings by his own people back home, so people in Texas knew he was serious.

Whoda thunk extra restrictions and more taxes would make people mad? After a series of neo-conservative Tea Party rallies orchestrated by Fox News failed, Texans decided to rebel. Sam Houston, who had just snuck across the border from Tennessee, was chosen to lead the rebellion. Others involved were William Barret Travis, Jim Bowie, Davy Crockett, James Fannin, and James Bonham. Fox News declared all was lost, while MSNBC claimed better days were ahead. Or vice-versa.

Declaring enough was enough, Santa Anna sent 5,000 Mexican troops into Texas in February of 1836. By the 23$^{rd}$, they were in San Antonio and ready to take back the Alamo. Yes, take back the Alamo. They had it first.

The Alamo (the Spanish word for cottonwood, the junky tree that fills the air with seeds floating on white fuzzy parachutes that are far too easy to inhale up a nostril) had been built by the Spanish in 1718 or so. Officially the Mission San Antonio de Valero, it was built on the cheap without an engineer. The church roof collapsed before the paint was dry, and the roof was never repaired and properly finished.

> *You may all go to Hell, and I will go to Texas.*
> *– Davy Crockett, Honorary Texan*

In 1833, Santa Anna had sent over a thousand soldiers with 21 cannons to fortify the Alamo and turn it into a real fort. Unfortunately, he put his brother-in-law in charge, probably because his wife begged him to give her poor, misunderstood brother a job. "All he needs is a chance, one little break, can't you do that for family?" she cried, but in Spanish.

Santa Anna must have already planned to attack Texas, because he ordered his schmuck brother-in-law, General Martin de Cos, to turn the ragged Alamo into the strongest Mexican military installation north of the Rio Grande. Cos did this.

Unfortunately, Santa Anna forgot to send brains, expertise, or a set of balls with his brother-in-law. In December 1835, 400 Texans led by Ben Milam attacked Cos in San Antonio. Three days later, Cos waved the white flag.

The 400 Texans suffered 19 casualties. Yes, only 19 Texan casualties to capture 1,100 men, a fortified Alamo, and 21

11

cannons. Only in Texas does 400 beat 1,100.

Determined to fix the mess his brother-in-law created, Santa Anna's 5,000 strong army surrounded the Alamo and shelled the Texans inside regularly for thirteen days. The rebels fought back, but ammunition ran low, and the men inside started to save as much as possible for the pending assault. They knew Santa Anna planned to take no prisoners because he flew a red flag in the tower of the San Fernando church not far away.

The attack came on March 6, 1836, at about five in the morning. Ninety minutes later, the battle ended. Every man in the Alamo was dead, but so were about 1,500 Mexican soldiers. Unfortunately, Santa Anna brought 5,000, and even in Texas, 189 can't beat 5,000. The only survivors were some women, children, and a servant or two.

Things continued going downhill for the Texas rebellion until April 21, 1836. Sam Houston and an army of just over 900 men outmaneuvered Santa Anna and attacked with the now famous cry, "Remember the Alamo!" Houston's army lost two soldiers, the Mexican army lost 630, and chains adorned the evil dictator Santa Anna.

> *My actions at the Alamo are justified as is my participation in them.*
>
> *– Santa Anna, Dishonorable Texan*

Remember the song *The Yellow Rose of Texas*? Meet Emily Morgan, or Emily West according to some, who was a mixed race slave girl who had been captured and forced into service in the General's household. While Sam Houston and his men surrounded the Mexican troops, Santa Anna was supposedly "entertaining" young Emily. That story about Santa Anna napping? Politically correct revisionist history to hide the fact Santa Anna was caught with his, ahem, pants down. And some believe Emily Morgan (the more popular name in the history books) was trained as a spy and placed in the General's company. Tricky, those early Texans.

People tend to forget the accompanying yell, "Remember Goliad!" in honor of a battle two weeks after the Alamo. Santa Anna captured, then executed, nearly 400 Texas soldiers at Goliad. Unlike Santa Anna, Houston didn't murder the soldiers he captured. Not even Santa Anna, who certainly deserved it.

Some historians believe Houston spared Santa Anna because they were both Masons, and Santa Anna gave the secret distress signal. That level of conspiracy paranoia staggers the imagination. Most likely, Houston, an honorable man, spared Santa Anna and expected him to behave honorably in return. Joke's on you, Sam.

The good news is, when you capture the dictator of the country you're fighting, you win. Texas won, and made official their Declaration of Independence from Mexico signed just four days before the Alamo was lost. And with Santa Anna captured, about one million square miles of territory changed hands from Mexico to Texas.

## The Republic of Texas

One might think it a bit overconfident for a rebellion to hold a constitutional convention starting a week after a huge military force surrounded their only fort, but that's what Texans did on March 1, 1836. By March 2, 1836, the Declaration of Independence was signed. Based on words and ideals cribbed from John Locke and Thomas Jefferson, some say George Childress, the leader of the committee, had written much of it before the meeting. The Texas Hysterical Society says being prepared is always a good thing, and three cheers for George Childress and the Texans who quickly signed the Declaration to announce the new Republic, then grabbed their weapons to create the new Republic.

Three more cheers for Sam Houston, the first President of the Republic of Texas. Larger than the Texas of today, the

Republic included parts of New Mexico, Oklahoma, Kansas, Colorado, and Wyoming. Look at the current Texas panhandle and imagine if it was twice as wide and twice as high wandering toward the northwest, and you'll have an idea of the size and scope of the Republic of Texas.

Mexico, for obvious reasons, didn't really accept the new Republic, even though we'd captured (but not killed) Santa Anna. His opponents back in Mexico declared him no longer president, meaning the treaty he'd signed to release Texas from Mexican control was not valid. Being nice, we sent Santa Anna back to Mexico rather than treating him liked he'd treated the soldiers in the Alamo and at Goliad. He later attacked Texas again in 1842, and then started the Mexican American War in 1846. Pesky fellow, that Santa Anna, and pretty darned ungrateful that we didn't string him up when we had the chance.

> *Texas, to be respected must be polite. Santa Anna living, can be of incalculable benefit to Texas; Santa Anna dead, would just be another dead Mexican.*
> *– Sam Houston, #1 Honorary Texan*

Times were tough in the budding "Empire of Texas" that some felt had been created. A few citizens felt a bit grandiose, even if the Texas version of the Palace of Versailles, the crown jewel of French royalty, was a doublewide log cabin. Yes, a log cabin on a mud street. That didn't stop President Sam Houston from looking presidential in a velvet coat and trousers highlighted by gold lace.

With no money and no respect, Texas elected their next president partly because of his rich sounding name: Mirabeau Buonaparte Lamar. Doesn't that name reek of regal? And President Lamar (oops, that sounds ordinary), er, King Mirabeau thought the executive doublewide mansion had a secret treasury filled with gold, but alas, no such luck. But really, could a man named Mirabeau Buonaparte really be expected to stay within a budget?

## The Pig War of 1841

Give King Mirabeau credit: he convinced the French to recognize the Republic of Texas in spite of the Austin Pig War of 1841. No, this is real, not a joke. Look it up in a reputable history book if you remain dubious. You won't hurt our feelings.

French envoy to the Republic of Texas Alphonse Dubois de Saligny became a bit vexed when pigs belonging to hotelkeeper Richard Bullock ate food for his horses, snuck into his house, and even invaded his bedroom. Horror of horrors, pigs in his bedroom did what pigs are wont to do (not that): eat things, including linens and papers. Dubois de Saligny ordered his servant to kill those pesky pigs, which vexed Richard Bullock.

Bullock, being Texan, did what came naturally, and beat the servant with a stick. Then he threatened the esteemed envoy of the French Empire with the same stick, and maybe a second stick for good measure. Dubois de Saligny, doing what the French do, backed down (sorry, that's a cheap joke at the expense of the French, the hardiest warriors the modern world has ever seen. After all, their motto is Fight Forever, Surrender Never).

Going all modern, Dubois de Saligny whined, then complained in his blog, and then complained to the Powers That Be of the Texas Republic. Unfortunately for him, he'd already pissed off the Powers That Be, and being Texan, they told him to go stuff himself, or get his own stick and fight Bullock like a man.

Throwing a major French hissy fit, Dubois de Saligny broke relations with the Republic of Texas and ran off to the French-friendly environs of Louisiana. Every now and then he'd pop up and yell at Texas some more about their horrible fate soon to come at the hands of World Power France.

Turns out Dubois de Saligny also pissed off the French Powers That Be as well. Officially, the French couldn't condone threatening their envoy with a stick, although they whispered later they wished they'd thought of that solution. Officially, they let the matter drop. So ended the global repercussions after some Texas pigs invaded a French pig's bedroom.

## *Independence*

His purpose in life of thwarting the French accomplished, President Mirabeau Buonaparte Lamar lost the next election to revolving door President Sam Houston. The list of Presidents of the Republic of Texas is:

**David G. Burnet** (interim)
    March 16, 1836 – October 22, 1836
**Sam Houston**
    October 22, 1836 – December 10, 1838
**Mirabeau Buonaparte Lamar**
    December 10, 1838 – December 13, 1841
**Sam Houston** (2nd term)
    December 13, 1841 – December 8, 1844
**Anson Jones**
    December 9, 1844 – February 19, 1846.

How did Texas make it through those rough 10 years between independence from Mexico and admission to the United State? Being tough on French envoys aside, we got lucky.

Sam Houston, hardened by his own troubles in Tennessee and Washington D.C. before coming to Texas, was a tough old bird strong enough to keep the rather shabby Republic of Texas from falling apart. Texans then and now dream big, and big dreamers found Texas a good place to put their dreams into action. Finally, Mexico had their own problems and didn't fully commit to recapturing their wayward northern territory. This allowed Sam Houston to cut defense spending and gave him time to cool down Texas big dreamers who wanted to declare war on Mexico.

Goodness, think if Texas had gathered the army needed and marched south, chanting, "Remember the Alamo" with every step. After all, we'd beaten Santa Anna before, and he was back big into Mexican politics, leading the fight against some French incursions. Texans could have taken advantage of the distraction and swept through Mexico down to South America.

Imagine a Republic of Texas that stretched from the Yucatan Peninsula north. Taking over Mexico would have given Texas all the Mexican territories to the west out to California and north up to the Canadian border. Not only would Texas be larger than Alaska, Texas would be bigger than the United States before buying Alaska. What an alternative history field day that idea presents.

Grandiose dreams aside, the Republic of Texas was a pretty rough place. Few women and fewer doctors made life dreary and short. The women who did come to Texas were strong, hardy, and self-sufficient. They are the same today. If you don't believe that, make one mad and see what happens. Good luck with that. And get well soon.

Towns were nothing but mud streets and log cabins. Men lived rough, drank too much on weekends and holidays, and mail service was awful. Wait, that's the way it still is today. Never mind.

> *I do not fight downhill.*
> *— Sam Houston, #1 Honorary Texan*
> *Said by six foot plus tall Sam when challenged*
> *to a duel by five foot one inch David Burnet.*

Sam Houston convinced the United States to recognize the Republic of Texas on March 3, 1837. Houston signed the treaty, but President Lamar approved the Lone Star flag in January 1839. Yes, the Texas state flag is the same as the Republic of Texas flag.

Lamar also picked Austin as the state capital after killing a bull on what became Congress Avenue in modern Austin, near the Colorado River. Since Congress Avenue leads to the State Capital offices, much more bull of the political variety has flowed over the decades. Too bad we can't use the State Capital bull manure as fertilizer.

Sam Houston preferred moving the state capital to Houston (some favoritism you think?) and then Washington-on-the-Brazos, where the Texas Declaration of Independence was signed. But when he tried to move all the state's papers out of Austin to keep them away from a division of the Mexican Army causing trouble in San Antonio, the bureaucrats of Austin refused. Led by Ms. Angelina Eberly, the bureaucrats fired a cannon to stop the papers from being taken. Remember that line about how tough Texas women were a few paragraphs ago? Firing cannons at men with marching orders from Sam Houston himself was all in a day's work for Ms. Eberly.

After a few more shots at Brushy Creek, Houston's men returned the papers to Austin, where they were safe when the city was once again made the state capital, this time for good. Hence the bureaucrat's creed: Paper Uber Alles.

Told you Texas women were tough. If you give one a cannon, prepare to pay the consequences.

## We're Number 28!

Many Texans felt folding Texas into the United States would solve many of the problems, such as lack of development, Indian wars, and that pesky Santa Anna. Sam Houston tried his entire second term to get the US interested, but the slavery issue made things tough. Northern states didn't want another slave state added.

Remember that the popular poker game today is "Texas Hold'em" not "Massachusetts Hold'em," although then Republic of Texas President Anson Jones was from the Bay State. Poker talent showed up early in Texas, and we bluffed ourselves into the United States.

> *Texas could exist without the United States but the United States cannot, without great hazard, exist without Texas.*
> — *Sam Houston, #1 Honorary Texan*

Texas made friends with several European countries, but most tellingly, England. America was still busy arguing with England about disputes new and old, and the idea of Texas as an English territory won over the fear of another slave state.

The United States and Texas signed the Treaty of Annexation on December 29, 1845 (Merry Christmas – now unwrap Texas). Paperwork delayed the official transfer of authority until February 19, 1846. The Republic of Texas was no more.

No, Texas cannot secede from the United States and become its own country once again. This nonsense got started up again in April 2009 when Texas Governor Rick Perry made those ah, curious statements to one of the Tea Party rallies in Austin. To be fair, Governor Perry is known more for his hair than his mastery of history, and Tea Party rallies are big on hyperbole (as are most political rallies). One might expect, however, that the governor of a state should know at least some history of said state. Hey, Gov, check out the Supreme Court *Texas v. White* ruling from 1869 that effectively killed the doctrine of state sovereignty.

The quality of Texas politicians has certainly dropped since the days of Sam Houston. On the other hand, if the tabloid reporters and the Internet existed in the early 1800s, outraged citizens might have run Sam Houston and all the other founders out of town on a rail. For that matter, the same would have happened to the Founding Fathers if paparazzi followed Thomas Jefferson and Ben Franklin around.

Joining the United States (We're number 28! *Yeah!*) didn't solve the problems in Texas. The streets were still muddy, the Indians still attacked, and Santa Anna kept making trouble. The difference was that we had more troops to go blast that pesky pegleg dictator – he lost a leg in a battle with the French in 1838, which we did in the Mexican-American War of 1846-1848. Remember that officially, the United States has only declared war five times (the War of 1812, this Mexican-American War, the Spanish-American War, World War I (the first War to End All Wars) and World War II (the second War to End All Wars). So this Mexican-American War, is, historically, a big deal.

Ever wonder if President James K. Polk regretted annexing Texas? He takes in the state and a war starts over the new star on the flag two months later. But Polk had a mandate to acquire both Texas and the Oregon Country, and if a war was what it took to keep Texas, it was worth it.

The United States military, fortified with plenty of Texans, including Texas Rangers, found itself standing in Mexico City in September of 1847. Santa Anna, the Mexican dictator once again, regularly lost battles when he had the Americans and Texans outnumbered three to one. Perhaps the General's Union should revoke his license.

Since Mexico City was under American control, it took a while for the government to reform so they could immediately surrender. That they did in February 1848, surrendering not only any claims to their former Texas territory but most of the rest of their holdings in what is now the western part of the United States, including California. Remember, when Mexicans sneak across the border and go to California, they're not illegal immigrants as much as people returning to the home of their ancestors.

> *Remember that whatever may be said by a lady or her friends, it is not part of conduct of a gallant or generous man to take up arms against a woman.*
> *— Sam Houston, #1 Honorary Texan*

American also threw in $15 million dollars for all the territory. Imagine, just about everything from Texas to the west and north to the Pacific Ocean or Canada for $15 mil. Today that might buy only one or two of the houses in Malibu overlooking that same Pacific Ocean.

The American flag became the fifth to fly over Texas, and things were, well, still miserable. But people had hopes, including one Austin resident who looked over the muddy Congress Avenue and wrote, "The city of Austin bids fair to become one of the most refined and pleasant cities in the western world." No one knows what he was smoking, but a hundred and some years later, most people feel Austin has become one of the nicest cities around. And now the streets are paved.

Central Texas around Austin was healthier than Houston, with their typical tropical sicknesses, and the northern and western areas of the state with little water. In fact, the little town of Wimberly in the Hill Country not too far from Austin was so healthy they had to shoot two people to start their cemetery.

## French Communists Invade Dallas

Don't tell Senator McCarthy, but communism started in Europe around 1830, known first as "communal socialism." Hounded by various governments around Europe, the nascent communists laid low and looked for a place with open spaces, cheap land, and a love of freedom. Where else but Texas? They learned about our wonderful republic from lectures and writings in Germany by Price Solms Braunfels who had visited

Texas in 1844.

The first group of 33 young students, leading the way for a planned group of thousands, arrived in 1847 and made friends with the Comanches in Llano County. They named their town Bettina, after respected author Bettina von Arnim. Guess if they were big on Dickens the town would have been named Charles.

Alas, the drought of 1848 killed their crops, and, being ideologically pure communists, everyone worked when they pleased, meaning less and less. Carving a niche in a frontier doesn't mix well with ideologically pure communism, and things fell apart.

A group of French communists, the Icarians, arrived in 1849. This group went to north Texas near Denton Creek (close to the modern town of Justin). Unfortunately, the crooked land promoters forgot to build the cabins promised in their brochures and on their Web site video. The half that survived the winter split, some heading up to Illinois, and some to Dallas. Yes, Dallas, called Little D at the time (before Dallas got a good PR firm).

> *Just because a hen clucks doesn't mean you have an egg to harvest.*
>
> *— The Old Cowboy*

They planned to buy nearly 60,000 acres in West Texas, and the state promised to help them with loans. But to handle the arriving group of 200, the leader, Victor Considerant, needed land quick. Buyers in a hurry are always easy marks, and Considerant spent his entire bankroll on 2,000 acres in West Dallas in 1855. The group was full not of farmers, blacksmiths, carpenters, and other laborers, but dancers, musicians, watchmakers, professors, and other non-frontier type occupations.

Alas, the late winter of 1856 did in their crops planted

before the May cold snap that froze the Trinity River. As the weather warmed, the drought did the rest of the damage.

By 1865, only a few dozen were left, and the land and all belongings were foreclosed on and seized. The communists moved to Dallas proper. In fact, Reverchon Park in Dallas is named for one of them, Julien Reverchon. The colony, on the banks of the Trinity River, was called La Reunion, and the name stuck to the area. That's why the first basketball arena near downtown Dallas was named Reunion Arena.

Of course, if the communists had bought the land they wanted in West Texas on top of oil, the group would have become very capitalistic if they could have held out until the early 1900s. But Texas weather, helped by shady land promoters, doomed the communist invasion of the 1850s.

## The War of Northern Aggression

Life started to improve in the 1850s after the war with Mexico was over, the state boundaries were set, and more immigrants arrived from other states and Europe. Germans found a nice home in central Texas, where you can still see their influence today. In fact, Germans made up the largest single ethnic group of immigrants at the time, and were still the third largest ethnic class in the 1990 census.

Transportation improved, with railroads and stagecoaches connecting towns and cities. The state's permanent school fund received the first bit of government money: two million dollars. Today, the school fund often gets twice that much from the kindly legislators each year. King Mirabeau gets the thanks for pushing education, as he was all for it and has been called the Father of Texas Education.

In 1860, three quarters of the people in Texas were not native Texans. Oh, will the horrors of unchecked immigration never end?

The slavery issue continued to be divisive until Texans voted to secede from the United States in 1861. Flag number six, the Confederate flag, flew over Texas during the War of Northern Aggression. Sam Houston campaigned vigorously against secession and the Civil War, fearing it would cost untold lives and leave the South in ruins. Smart guy, Sam Houston. He deserves to have the biggest city in the state named after him.

> *It is admitted by all that the cultivated mind is the guardian genius of democracy and, while guided and controlled by virtue, is the noblest attribute of man. It is the only dictator that freemen acknowledge and the only security that freemen desire.*
> *— Mirabeau Buonaparte Lamar, Honorary Texan (and second President of the Republic of Texas)*

Thousands of Texas soldiers never returned from battles up north. Food, supplies, clothes, and even coffee became nearly impossible to find after Union ships blockaded the Gulf of Mexico. On June 19, 1865, a Union general and 1800 soldiers landed in Galveston and declared that all slaves were free. "Juneteeth" remains a major holiday for many even today.

War's aftermath, chaos, ruled the day as Texas wasn't officially a state anymore, and the Confederate government, weak as it was, disbanded and left an authority vacuum. Since nature abhors a vacuum but greed loves opportunity, Yankees descended on Texas like a plague of locusts with strange accents, and acted like dictators. They took control of business in the state, making fortunes by shady dealings with their friends at the expense of the public. They were called carpetbaggers then. Today they go by the titles investment banker and Wall Street executive.

These two-legged locusts were called carpetbaggers because of the type of soft-sided suitcases many carried. If there had been carpet in those days, they would have stolen that, too. As it was, the carpetbag suitcases carried away everything of value the Texans hadn't already lost during the deprivations of war. Maybe we should have a seventh state flag: a green background with a white dollar sign.

## *Round'em Up, Cowboy*

Luckily, even the largest carpetbag suitcase couldn't carry a longhorn steer. Left over from cattle abandoned by Mexican ranchers when Texas became independent in 1836, wild cattle, including some with the trademark wide, wide horns, roamed around large parts of the state. The market in Texas wasn't good, because the cattle were close and plentiful, but people back east wanted some of that good Texas beef. Thus began the cattle drives popularized on western movies and TV shows for several decades.

Unfortunately for the Hollywood casting directors, cowboys of the time didn't look like Marion Morrison, the famous Western action hero from Iowa you may know as John Wayne. If you had taken a census of cowboys in 1880, which you couldn't because they were riding around chasing cows, the race check boxes would be predominantly Indian, with African American and Hispanic the next most popular. Popular Indian groups for cattle drives included the Pawnee and Osage tribes. Sorry, John Wayne, but for cowboys of the time, the name John was far less popular than the name Juan.

Mavericks have been in the news for years, and not just the Dallas Maverick basketball team. Samuel Augustus Maverick, who settled around San Antonio before Texas split from Mexico, gave us the label. The rule was to brand your cattle (and there are some fascinating brands and stories behind them) so you could identify them. Samuel didn't, perhaps because he was lazy or scared of PETA suing him for hurting his cows, and thereupon claimed any unbranded cattle as mavericks and therefore his.

The same attitude exists today as some politicians claim to be "unbranded and free" and deserve to be called a maverick.

Unfortunately for them, Texans know mavericks don't do the work they should, expect everyone else to do their work for them, and then loudly proclaim themselves leaders. Of what? Not doing your work doesn't make you a leader, it makes you a joke.

> *I believe that if life gives you lemons, you should make lemonade. And try to find somebody whose life has given them vodka, and have a party.*
>
> *– Ron White*

Cattle ranchers sent two drives a year from Texas up to Kansas and the railroad connections they needed to get their cattle to the east. Pay was about a dollar per day and room and board, which on cattle drives meant chuck wagon meals and a blanket on the ground. Leading cowboys often got bonuses or a bit of profit sharing.

Alas for Hollywood and cow-oriented nostalgia, the cowboy era faded as fences blocked the cattle drive routes, and the trains discovered Texas and came to the cattle instead of the other way around. The cowboy mystique lives on and will for generations more. Turns out cowboy hats still block the sun well, and cowboy boots work on pickups just as well as horses.

The Indian mystique didn't do so well. A combination of the United States Army forcing Indians off their land, and buffalo hunters killing a critical source of food, moved the Indians away from their historic home places. Government treaties, broken more often than a carpetbagger's promise, pushed the Indians to small areas called reservations.

Today people go to pay homage to the Indian way of life by losing money in casinos. But not in Texas where the Lottery Lobbyists have successfully stopped the casinos. How the Lottery Lobbyists convinced the Legislature that the insanely bad odds of the Texas Lottery is not gambling, while casinos are, remains a mystery. However, that's the kind of mystery campaign finance reform laws address.

The new 20th century closed out what many consider the "real" Texas of cowboys, Indians, and the open range. September 1900 also closed out almost all of Galveston, as a hurricane swept over Galveston Island and the city of Galveston, home to 37,000 residents, killing thousands. In September 2008, Hurricane Ike scoured Galveston Island clean once again and flooded the shoreline city of Galveston. At least the trailer parks on modern Galveston Island were destroyed by a hurricane rather than the cliché of a tornado, although we doubt that made them feel any better.

> *One tequila, two tequila, three tequila... floor. Tequila first came to the United States through El Paso in 1873. Don Cenobio Sauza sent three barrels over from Mexico, no doubt to a fraternity party.*

## *War, Depression, War*

Over 200,000 Texans served in the First World War (once known optimistically as The War To End All Wars), and 5,170 Texan solders and one female nurse were killed. During the War, in 1918, women were finally allowed to vote thanks to a bill introduced by John Morris Sheppard, a Congressman from Texas. The year earlier he had introduced a bill establishing Prohibition. Luckily, only one of his bills stuck.

The Texas Senate, rightfully upset at the sinking of the Cunard cruise ship *Lusitania* off the coast of Ireland in May 1915 by a German submarine (even though the Germans announced they were going to sink the ship in the New York newspapers), introduced a resolution asking the United States to sever diplomatic relations with Germany. Add in the fact that the Germans kept trying to trick Mexico into declaring war on the US to distract us from WWI, and you can see why Texans were unhappy with the Germans.

Good thing that pesky Santa Anna wasn't still around or he might have declared war on the U.S. once again, this time while carrying German rifles and maybe those funny helmets with the spike on top. And Germany's pledge to help Mexico reclaim the lands lost to the U.S., mainly Texas, was just the type of offer to get Santa Anna excited. But the constant threat at the border gave military commanders some practice, and inflamed the population. As a result, nearly a million Texas men registered for the military draft.

General and future President Dwight David Eisenhower, born in Denison on October 14, 1890, received the Distinguished Service Medal for his work during the First World War. Eisenhower heard about the attack on Pearl Harbor when his wife Mamie woke him up from a nap in their quarters at Fort Sam Houston in San Antonio.

Before that fateful nap, Texas and the world struggled through the Great Depression, an appropriate name because hearing just a little about the conditions of the time is enough to depress anyone. One of every five manufacturing plants in Texas closed, throwing almost as many people out of work as the horrible farming conditions.

> *Don't squat with your spurs on.*
> *— The Old Cowboy*

During the 1930s, farmers in some areas could barely farm because their dirt blew away. Yes, the Dust Bowl is a real catastrophic environmental event, not another football game around New Year's Day. "Black Blizzards" full of dirt blew topsoil as far away as New York City. Over 100 million acres in Texas and other states were part of the affected area. In Amarillo in 1935, there were seven days with zero visibility, including one stretch where the dust was so bad people couldn't see for eleven straight hours.

Finally, there was a bit of Texas on Broadway. In fact, the

dust went past Broadway. As far as 500 miles out to sea, ships reported black dust settling on their decks.

A bit of Texas 1930s crime became Hollywood fodder. Bonnie and Clyde, gorgeous and dashing in the 1967 movie, were in reality vicious, cowardly, depraved, and thoroughly unbeautiful in real life. Hmm, maybe they were more Hollywood than we thought, but that's a subject for the tabloids and gossipy websites, not the Texas Hysterical Society (unless you ask really nicely).

Times were tough in Texas and around the world during the Depression. Over 300,000 Texans received some assistance from the Federal Emergency Relief Administration. Over 110,000 were employed by the Civilian Conservation Corps. Thousands more received their paychecks, sometimes for the first time in years, from the National Recovery Administration and Works Projects Administration. Take a close look at the small bridges you pass over in the more rural areas, and you'll often see a WPA logo. Take a real close look and you may actually see water under the bridge.

> *When I was a kid in Houston, we were so poor we couldn't afford the last two letters – we were just po!*
> *– George Foreman*

More noticeable WPA improvements include the Main Building at the University of Texas, and much of the River Walk in San Antonio. Nice of the WPA to provide the UT students a cool place to visit (perhaps for parties?) in San Antonio.

World War II, maybe more than the New Deal programs, finally pulled Texas and the rest of the country out of the Great Depression. As always, Texans responded to the call to duty, and more than 750,000 Texans wore one uniform or another during the war. The government put fifteen military bases in the state (lots of room to spread out, and few bad weather days to disrupt training). There are also several prisoner of war camps located in the state, although we assume "room to spread out" wasn't a consideration for the prisoners.

War and oil always go together (and sometimes war for oil, official protestations notwithstanding), and the Texas oil business got a huge boost from the war. Houston in particular developed their refinery business, including Shell Oil, building an explosives chemical refinery in the record time of four months. Refineries make more than oil, you know. In fact, half the synthetic rubber used by the various services came from Texas (that's rubber, singular).

Nearly a billion (with a B) dollars of refinery capacity, new and expanded, took place in the Houston area during and right after the war. The area between Houston, Freeport, and Port Arthur became one of the two largest petrochemical refining areas in the country, and remains a critical provider of refined products to this day.

> *Everyone has something to teach, and everyone has something to learn. Too bad those folks don't match up very often.*
>
> *– The Old Cowboy*

Even though natural gas was just an annoying oil-drilling byproduct early on, by the middle of the war it became important for heating, particularly in the northeast. So critical, in fact, that the government built a 1,300 mile pipeline from Texas to West Virginia to move the gas up there. Glad they finally figured out how to use the gas, because oil drillers were just burning it off from wells, called flaring. The state didn't put a stop to that waste until 1949. Now if the state could only put a stop to the wasted time and effort spent by the Legislature, things would be wonderful.

Texas hadn't been big in shipbuilding because the coastline gradually slopes off into the Gulf of Mexico, and shipbuilders like deep-water harbors. But the war effort demanded ships, so the Neches River Ship Channel at Beaumont was deepened, and shipbuilding commenced. Todd Shipyards used modern manufacturing techniques and cut the time to build a ship from 254 days down to 53, and turned out 222 ships. Brown Shipbuilding Company produced more than 300. Several hundred million dollars in ship contracts kept the Texas coast busy until the war ended, and employment dropped from 35,000 to fewer than 4,500 in 1963. Shame to lose that many good Texas swabbees, but that's what happens when a war ends (and that's really a good thing, despite the unemployment).

But things weren't too bad, because Houston was the fastest growing city in the country in 1948. In fact, Houston had more than doubled in size over the 1940s. Huge military contracts will do that to a town. San Antonio grew more than 60 percent, also largely due to military and government money. Austin increased 50 percent.

Dallas and Fort Worth each got airplane plants and big contracts during the war, and both cities continued to benefit from the wartime manufacturing base for decades. Ford built a plant in Dallas not far from Fair Park. Each car produced there had a decal on the back window that said, "Made in Texas by Texans."

> *If I'm in a suit, somebody better be in a casket.*
> *– The Old Cowboy*

In 1950, 60 percent of Texans lived in the cities, and the state population had grown by 20 percent (seems a small number considering all the growth in Houston, doesn't it?) But people kept coming for many reasons, including some that were out of this world.

The Soviet space program caught Americans by surprise when they started flinging rockets into orbit in 1957. Not to be outdone in sending brave astronauts into space in dangerous rockets, the Manned Space Center opened in 1957 about 30 miles south of Houston. Today, the 142 buildings and 19,000 plus workers at the Lyndon B. Johnson Space Center comprise one of nine NASA (National Aeronautics and Space Administration) locations around the country.

Helping the space program and everything else electronic was Jack Kilby. As a relatively new employee at Texas Instruments in Dallas he didn't qualify for a two-week summer vacation. While everyone else was gone, Kilby figured out how to make transistors (invented by AT&T researchers a decade earlier), cheap enough to use in a variety of products. The semiconductor was born. See how much work can get done with management isn't around to bother the employees? Give a smart man time to think without being over-managed, and great things happen. Since then, TI has only made about 750 Gazillion transistors. And Kilby made a huge step in reducing the cost of transistors, built with silicon (made of processed sand), by about a million to one, making the modern world possible.

> *The Frozen Margarita machine was invented by Dallas restaurant owner Mariano Martinez in 1971. Over 36,000 gallons of frozen tequila drinks were sold the first year. Today, over 60 percent of all tequila goes into margaritas, frozen or otherwise, mostly ordered by sorority girls getting ready for fraternity parties.*

The period after World War II until about 1982 was a Texas explosion burning brightly over the heads of fellow Americans and the entire world. Everyone's favorite oil villain, J. R. Ewing (Larry Hagman), ruled the TV airwaves in *Dallas* the nighttime soap opera. Willie Nelson and Janis Joplin ruled the radio airwaves, and Willie's "Red Headed Stranger" album in 1975 defined the new "outlaw country" movement. The TV and music made Texas look that much bigger and grander as the Texas myths continued to intrigue the world outside our fair borders.

1982 saw a double whammy of oil prices plummeting (thanks to speculators) and real estate imploding in the Savings and Loan scandal (banks and financial "geniuses" running amok). While Texas took a breath before the next big growth spurt, the idea of Texas as somewhere bigger, better, and bolder than the rest of the world took hold in the minds of people the world over.

By the mid to late 1980s, Houston, Dallas, Fort Worth, Austin, and San Antonio had vibrant downtown areas devoid of people as the suburbs became the place to be. More than the residents abandoned downtowns. In 1988, three quarters of the available office space in Houston was outside the traditional downtown area. Dallas could have three downtowns: the traditional one, Las Colinas, and north of Dallas spread across Richardson, Addison, and Plano.

> *You know, when it comes to garbage, people want us to pick it up, but they don't want us to put it down again, particularly near their house.*
> *— Houston Mayor Louie Welch*

Don't make the mistake of believing the administration in these cities are ignoring the problems of urban sprawl and the dependence on expensive cars and their expensive oil and their dependence on their expensive roads. Each city regularly organizes a committee to get a grip on the sprawl and provide a coherent plan for the future. Smart people make smart recommendations full of wonderful solutions to current problems. The city politicians take the documents happily, then immediately bury them in the back yard so they'll never have to look at them again.

Of course growth continued, more people came to Texas,

and the place got a little messy. In another example of Texas being #1 in the wrong thing, the Houston Ship Channel was voted the most polluted body of water in the country, particularly when rain flushed all the overflow sewage and chemical run off down and out to the Gulf.

Think football isn't important in Texas? Governor Bill Clements won his first term in 1986. Right after he took office, investigations linked Clements to a scheme paying football players at SMU. Clements' reputation suffered, and the SMU football team got the "death penalty," a very Texan name for the drastic measure of shutting down the football team for a year. At least it wasn't a real death penalty, and SMU decided to keep the program shuttered a second year because they couldn't find enough experienced players.

As the 80s moved into the 90s, Texans started to address the sprawl the openness of Texas encouraged, as cities gave way to suburbs as far as the car could drive. Cities started to get a bit more organized, except for Houston, a town proud of placing no limits on growth and land use by passing pesky government zoning ordinances. The majority of Texans now live in urban, rather than rural areas, although outsiders still ask natives living in the suburbs where they keep their horses. And we answer proudly, "under the hoods of our cars and trucks."

## Official State Things

The pecan was designated as the official Texas State Tree in 1919. That makes sense, because we have millions of pecan trees in Texas. What's curious is why the pecan wasn't designated the official Texas State Nut until 2001. Maybe the politicians wanted to keep the Texas State Nut designation for themselves.

It wasn't until 1993 that the horned lizard (horned frog or horny toad to natives) was elected the official Texas State Reptile. Obviously, the horny toad lobby finally bought their way into the State Reptile spotlight.

Hot and spicy chili is the official Texas State Dish, so proclaimed in 1977. This surprised many Texans, especially the menfolk who assumed the official Texas State Dish was any member of the Dallas Cowboys Cheerleaders. Really, State Dish committee members, chili over Cheerleaders? If chili is the Texas State Dish, can the Cheerleaders become the official Texas State Dishes?

Perhaps the chili choice has something to do with rodeo being chosen the official Texas State Sport in 1997. It appears that the Dallas Cowboys having the Cheerleaders and multiple Super Bowl trophies wasn't enough to convince the committee to make football the official Texas State Sport.

On the other hand, the rodeo does have death-defying clowns. It must be hard to tell clowns who face down rampaging bulls "no" when they come to your office to lobby for the rodeo.

In 1930, Texas officially adopted a state motto: Friendship. Perhaps someone should have reminded the Official State Motto Committee that a motto tends to be a phrase, not a word.

*Contrary to popular belief, not every native Texan rides horses and shoots guns. Jasper D. in Houston has never been on a horse, and Lorraine S. in Beaumont has never shot a gun (but she's only six, so give her time).*

## Six Flags Over ... Texlahoma?

Yes, there was almost a Texlahoma in the early 1900s, but not for the reason you think. Texas didn't threaten to conquer Oklahoma like they almost did Mexico more than a half a century earlier. This all came about because of cars and a lack of road funding.

The car was becoming the new horse and buggy and drivers wanted much better roads. But the folks in northern

Texas and western Oklahoma were far, far away from their respective state capitals. They were obviously too poor to "lobby" their politicians as well, so their road building budgets looked as flat as West Texas.

Oklahoman A. P. Sights suggested 46 counties in Texas and 23 in Oklahoma split and form their own new state. The *New York Times* started paying attention, and why not? Texas and Arkansas already had a city straddling their state line, Texarkana, so why not another stupid name starting with Texas?

The U. S. vice president at the time, Texan John Nance Gardner IV, already thought carving Texas into multiple states was a good idea. After all, that would give the Texas area that many more Senators and therefore more influence in Washington D. C.

Unfortunately for the veep, Texans realized that if they split up the state, or if a section seceded and glommed onto some of Oklahoma, they couldn't call themselves Texans anymore. End of discussion.

Veep Gardner earned the best, and most Texan, nickname for a veep ever: Cactus Jack. Seems another of his enlightened ideas for changing Texas government was to officially name the prickly pear cactus as the state flower. Alas for Cactus Jack, the equally beautiful but less painful bluebonnet won the state flower designation. But we doubt the winner would have wanted to be known as Bluebonnet Bill. Cactus Jack is a much better nickname.

# Business, Oil, and Money

> *Texas doesn't have recessions, but I must admit that this is the worst boom I've seen in years.*
>
> *– The Old Cowboy*

## Come and Listen to a Story 'Bout a Man Named... Patillo

Surprise – Texas wasn't the site of the first real oil well in the U.S. That distinction belongs to Titusville, Pennsylvania, in 1859.

At the turn of the 20th century, there were no SUVs with engines big enough to pass everything on the road except a gas station. Why not? Because Gottlieb Daimler (think Daimler Mercedes) and Wilhelm Maybach didn't invent the gasoline engine with vertical cylinders and a fuel injected carburetor until 1885. Oil was used for heating and lighting, and a few worthless tonic medicines, but the car market was pretty darn small.

In 1900, the Standard Oil Company, owned by John D. Rockefeller, controlled about 90 percent of American oil. But not in Texas, because no oil had been discovered there, at least officially. Clues popped up their heads like spring dandelions, such as Sour Springs near Beaumont, where smelly gasses and brown liquids gave the springs their name. In 1894, the city of Corsicana cursed the oil that got in the way of their well searching for artesian water.

We can't blame the good folks, or at least the good ancestors of folks, in Corsicana for ignoring the oil, because several founded the Corsicana Oil Company. Besides, the so-called "experts" claimed there were no significant oil deposits west of the Mississippi River.

> *Texas oilman's prayer: "Please, Lord, give us a nice oil boom. I promise I won't piss it away like I did the last three."*

Good thing Patillo Higgins didn't listen to that nonsense. Born in Sabine Pass, Texas, in 1863 (the middle of the Civil War), he was a self-taught geologist. Higgins was sure a salt dome hill four miles south of Beaumont covered an oil field. He spent time in Pennsylvania in 1889 learning about the oil business, so he had experience. But back home in Beaumont, everyone thought he was just a one-armed crazy guy with a wild past. He shot and killed a deputy in his misspent youth, but lost his right arm in the gunfight. Even though reformed and a deacon, yelling about oil all the time while waving his one arm made him look more than a little bit loony.

Higgins needed help transforming from fool to genius, and that help came in the person of Anthony Lucas (sometimes called Luchich), a Croatian engineer living in Washington D.C. Higgins couldn't convince Rockefeller and Standard Oil to buy the hill with the oil hiding underneath, but he convinced Lucas.

After learning the hard way about drilling in sandy soil while drilling water wells in Louisiana, Lucas had money and expertise. Matched with Higgins' knowledge of the area and geological knowledge, how could they lose?

Yet they did, for two years. Then three brothers, Jim, Curt, and Al Hamill of Corsicana (and the oil company there) brought in some other oil hands. Together, they convinced Andrew Mellon to shake loose some shekels to fund more drilling.

January 10, 1901, started out like any other day full of frustration at the oil derrick at Spindletop, except colder. Then a giant stream of mud flew high in the air, blowing out six tons of steel pipe and wrecking the derrick. After a little break spewing blue gas, the Spindletop oil well starting blowing oil 200 feet into the air. Texas entered the oil age, a source of much money and madness for the rest of the 20th century.

Texas didn't have the first oil well in the US, but they had the first gusher. An estimated 80,000 barrels of oil per day spewed everywhere, even killing crops on farms nearby. When the strong wind changed, oil reached houses and stores in Beaumont. The eruption continued for nine days.

> *"Hurry, Anthony, something awful has happened. The well is spouting!"*
> — Caroline Lucas, wife of Anthony Lucas.

Anthony Lucas became a hero, Andrew Mellon got richer, but Patillo Higgins was largely forgotten. This is how it goes, isn't it? You're a damn fool until suddenly you're a fracking genius. You get credit in the history books, but no money in the pocket.

Spindletop didn't produce a lot of oil for very long, but it drew oil people from all over the country, and convinced many in the area they were oil people, too. This set the stage for all the oil exploration across the state, especially in West Texas. When you have a chance, go to Lamar University's Spindletop-Gladys Boomtown Museum. Mouse potatoes, click on over to www.spindletop.org.

## Got Dirty Birds?

If you ever take a family car trip north on Interstate 35 from Temple to Waco, be prepared for your kids to start screaming, "Look, there's a dinosaur!" at Exit 315 for Bruceville / Eddy. When you whip your head around, you will see giant concrete statues of, yes, dinosaurs, as well as apes, angels, and yep, birdbaths.

I-35 Statuary has several acres of highway frontage that they use to advertise the concrete statues. Need a triceratops in your yard? You'll be the talk of the neighborhood. Don't worry, you don't have to strap it to the hood of your Honda, I-35 Statuary will either deliver statues or create them at your location.

Some statues are painted. Want a full color Snow White

and some Dwarves? A bright blue gorilla? You can have them, just pay with cash or check, not a credit card.

Originally, the location was the outlet store for Double D Statuary. Now separately owned, I-35 Statuary still carries plenty of Double D products as well as those from other companies, and the artworks they have created as well.

One of the areas of expansion has been into fiberglass. I-35 now sells an eight-foot tall fiberglass chicken. Why a fiberglass chicken? Because a concrete chicken is just silly.

Check out their website: gotdirtybirds.com, so named because they sell lots and lots of birdbaths.

## IT Means Infobahn Texas

Texas made news in 2006 in the area of public sector outsourcing of IT (Information Technology) needs. The deal was big ($863 million over seven years) but not Texas sized, because Virginia did one about the same time for 10 years and $1.3 billion (with a B for Billion). That's Texas sized, but alas, neither Texans nor Virginians are happy today.

How's this for a modern marriage – Texas started the deal in 2006, and by 2008 had suspended the contract for "service delivery problems." Issues that the state's leading information manager claimed were indications of IBM's inability to perform were slowdowns in the performance of state agencies like the DMV. And if you live in America, you know the Department of Motor Vehicles in every state exemplifies excellence in service. Wait, they exemplify the excellence in service shown in Communist Russia, and are now run by refugee bureaucrats who were exiled by the Communists for subpar performance. With this history, can we really blame IBM for lousy performance from our state agencies?

*There are no traffic jams on the extra mile.*
*– Roger Staubach, Honorary Texan*

According to our state agencies, everything is IBM's fault. The state has fined IBM $7.3 million for poor performance (too bad we can't fine the state agencies for poor performance). But the state has also paid $486.7 million, about half the total fee, since the contract is about halfway done.

The contract called for IBM to revamp 27 state agencies. By summer 2010, about four years in, five had been revamped and five more were in the process of being partially revamped. Doesn't take a genius to see that IBM is behind. The state contends IBM has upgraded only about 10 percent of the computer consolidation they are contracted for, leading the state to threaten dire consequences such as canceling the contract.

> *The best time to plant a tree was 20 years ago. In the event you didn't plant one then, the second-best time is today.*
> *– T. Boone Pickens, Honorary Texan*

If you're IBM, do you get nervous? You've got half your money already and have done 10 to 20 percent of the work. Calling it quits might be a great deal for IBM. And they wouldn't have to deal with any more bureaucrats, an added bonus.

Experts say these big public sector outsourcing deals have about the same problem rates as comparable big private sector deals. The main difference is how they handle the problems. In the private sector, the managers who drafted and signed the contract are held accountable. In public sector deals, bureaucrats are covered with Teflon, and none are accountable. They just start whining publicly to put pressure on the company, like Texas is doing to IBM right now.

Experts also say that states cause many of the problems through poor planning, poor management, and oversized expectations. Really? State bureaucrats aren't the sharpest quills on the porcupine?

States give the normal blather about finding the right technology partner, but the contracts always go to the lowest bidder. The most optimistic bidding company, who believes the problems aren't as bad as they look, and the system really isn't all geflugted because state IT management can't do their job, wins the bid. Then they realize the problems are as bad, or worse, than they thought, and state IT management bureaucrats can't but trusted to think far enough ahead to park their cars in the shade during a Texas summer. About a year or so into the contract, the honeymoon is over and the whining begins.

> *The difference between winning and losing is not quitting.*
> *– H. Ross Perot*

Don't forget that state buildings are full of bureaucrats, and all of them want to protect their phony baloney jobs (thank you, Mel Brooks and *Blazing Saddles*) by getting involved in the contract process. Each department head wants to feel important and so demands something special, or tries something clever to cut the cost to their department. For instance, they often refuse 24x7 technical support to ask for 23x7 to cut the cost. After all, what are the chances they'll need technical support at 3 A.M.?

No offense to lawyers (well, honestly, some offense), but you can't sue people into liking you more and doing a better job. Suing your outsourcing partners brings to mind that old poster from the 1970s showing a pirate ship and saying "The floggings will continue until morale improves." Remember – the people managing this contract for the state are people who believe meetings are productive work.

But every technology company knows they are invited in to be the whipping boy (there we are, back to floggings) so the state managers can claim nothing is their fault. Most of the time, they get away with this charade, but Virginia fired their chief manager in charge of their botched $1.3 billion (with a B) contract. So far, the major Texas state managers are still in charge. Feel better now? But don't worry about state managers fired for their outsourcing mistakes. Most of them get better jobs working as outsourcing consultants.

> *The only difference between a pigeon and the American farmer today is that a pigeon can still make a deposit on a John Deere.*
> *– Jim Hightower, Agriculture Commissioner of Texas, 1986.*

No matter how well you draft the contract terms and conditions, the outsourcing company can't fix the problems inside the state. Career bureaucrats who stopped learning about technology when Windows first went graphical will not become technical geniuses anytime soon. Managers who can barely decide what type of donuts to order for their meetings, the ones they have each morning for three hours asking why more progress isn't being made on critical projects, won't suddenly become decisive captains of bureaucracy. It's always much easier to blame the contractor, in this case IBM, than it is to look in the mirror.

Here's what will happen, based on history. The state will whine, IBM will threaten to countersue, and state managers will get nervous. Citizens, weighing IBM's reputation against that of state bureaucrats, will believe IBM's stories about lack of internal management and contradictory demands from bureaucrats.

If things go as usual, the contract will be expanded for a few hundred million dollars, and everyone will go away happy (except taxpayers). When this is all finished, your dealings with state bureaucracy, such as the DMV, will be fast, efficient, and pleasant. No, we can't say that with a straight face. Laugh with us.

## *Ranch to the Max*

Few things say "Texas Big" better than the King Ranch, now 825,000 acres covering all or part of Nueces, Keney, Klegerg, Brooks, Jim Wells, and Willacy counties. At one time the ranch was bigger than 1.2 million acres, or about the size of the Grand Canyon National Park. The King Ranch today stretches between Corpus Christi and Brownsville, is bigger than Rhode Island, and is one of the world's largest ranches.

Such excess wasn't in the cards when Richard King (born in New York City) met Mifflin Kenedy on the riverboat Kenedy captained. Richard King saw the land he would eventually buy when traveling from Brownsville to Corpus Christi for the Lone Star Fair, where he met another future partner, Texas Ranger Captain Gideon K. Lewis.

King and Lewis started a cow camp on Santa Gertrudis Creek, the area that caught King's eye on his trip. The partners bought up a Spanish land grant, Rincon de Santa Gertrudis, for $300 in 1853. The 15,500 acre start bumped up by another 53,000 acres when they bought the Garza Santa Gertrudis grant, although details are vague on whether they ever actually paid for the Garza land officially after waiting for titles to clear and inheritance rules to get clarified.

There were lots of deals made between partners buying and selling new plots and new partners buying into old plots. People died, causing more deals, especially when Gideon Lewis was killed by the husband of a woman with whom he was "friendly." Since there was murder involved, we can assume Lewis and the woman were very, very friendly.

> *Unofficial state motto: Don't mess with Texas... We're armed.*

One of the great stories of the King Ranch is that of the Mexican village Cruillas. During a severe drought in 1854,

45

King bought all the cattle from the desperate villagers. On the way home, he realized the village no longer had their cattle, and therefore no way to make a living. He went back and hired the entire village to move to the Ranch and work for him. This group became known as "King's Men" and some of the descendants still work on the Ranch today. Not only did the King Ranch offer a job for life, it offered a job for generations.

The Santa Gertrudis breed of cattle, a cross of Brahmans and Beef Shorthorns, was created on the King Ranch. The breed became the first American breed of beef cattle when they were officially recognized in 1940.

Depression times were bad for the King Ranch, just like they were bad for everyone. But not everyone had hundreds of thousands of acres of land sitting on top of oil, as the King Ranch did. Just before bad came to worse, the first oil lease was signed in 1919, but it ran out in 1926 without finding anything of value. A new lease was signed in 1933, paying the Ranch 13 cents per acre for drilling rights on 971,000 acres, plus 1/8th of every barrel pumped. Humble Oil struck oil and gas in 1939, but the discovery of the Borregas Oilfield in 1945 really turned up the heat. By 1953 there were 650 producing gas and oil wells on the property.

Now folks can visit the King Ranch Museum in the aptly named town of Kingsville. You can even buy a King Ranch edition of several Ford F-150 pickup models to carry home your souvenirs.

> *Ideas are a dime a dozen. People who implement them are priceless. Nothing great is ever accomplished without follow-through.*
>
> *– Mary Kay Ash*

## Neiman-Marcus Makes Dallas Fashionable

Since most stories about the founding of Neiman-Marcus

start with the move of the Marcus family from Atlanta to Dallas, many people don't know that Stanley Marcus was actually born in Dallas in April 1905. His father, Herbert Marcus Sr., and his aunt Carrie Marcus Neiman (married to Al Neiman), both worked in Dallas when Stanley was born. Herbert was the buyer for boy's clothing at Sanger Brothers, and Carrie an assistant buyer for A. Harris and Company.

Historical footnote: those two department store eventually merged into Sanger-Harris, a major mid-level department store strong in the Dallas area that expanded to Oklahoma, New Mexico, and Arizona. The Foley's chain ate Sanger-Harris in 1987, and they were later eaten by Macy's. Now back to Neiman-Marcus (and what is it about department stores and hyphens?)

Herbert Sr. and Carrie left their decent jobs in Dallas and moved to Atlanta to start their own company in the sales-promotion business. After a couple of years, they were doing so well they had two buyout offers: one for $25,000 cash, and the other for all rights in the state of Kansas for a new-fangled soft drink named Coca-Cola (another hyphen!). Stanley Marcus later always explained that Neiman-Marcus started "as a result of the bad judgment of its founders."

Hard to say that was really a bad decision, because Neiman-Marcus turned out pretty well. But the opening in September 10th during the Panic of 1907 was a bit of a downer for the three entrepreneurs, since there was a recession, Carrie was in the hospital recovering from a miscarriage, and Herbert Sr. was home with typhoid fever. Little Stanley, at only two years old, had his hands full with the opening chores. Wait, his uncle Al did most of the honors, not Stanley.

Stanley didn't jump into the sales business until age 10, when his parents put him on the sidewalk selling *Saturday Evening Post* subscriptions. But sales seeped into his blood from the full color photographs in the magazine, and he later made Neiman-Marcus famous the world over.

> *Texas weather forecast: Chili today, hot tamale.*

Rough start or not, the store was a winner from the beginning, and the handpicked merchandise Carrie brought in from New York sold out completely in a few weeks. Every customer was greeted by one of the owners as they entered the store, a level of personal service that helped Neiman-Marcus rise to the top quickly.

Unlike the other stores at the time that didn't serve the customer, didn't take returns, and didn't offer refunds, Neiman-Marcus did all of these. They treated the customers better than anyone ever had, and probably ever will again.

Anecdotes about the service made competitors shake their heads at how stupid the Neiman-Marcus folks were, like when Herbert Sr. let a woman return a dress after three months, and he gave her the full refund of $175 (that was more than a year's pay for many at the time). Herbert Sr. had the last laugh, as that customer, loyal to Herbert Sr. and Neiman-Marcus, spent well over $500,000 with the store in later years. After expanding the store in 1914 after a fire completely destroyed their original location, Neiman-Marcus made a profit of more than $40,000 on sales of $700,000, nearly double the sales in the original, smaller, location.

Stanley Marcus took over the company after his father Herbert Sr. died in 1950, and his aunt Carrie died two years later (Al divorced Carrie and cashed out of the family business for a cool quarter million in 1928). Since he'd joined the store in 1920 (but he did take a break for college), Stanley had spent plenty of time learning the secrets of outstanding customer service from his father.

> *The first hotel owned by Conrad Hilton was purchased in Cisco, Texas, during the oil boom in 1919. The first Hilton hotel built from scratch opened in Dallas in 1925.*

Listen to one of the crazy business ideas Stanley used to grow Neiman-Marcus: in 1936, for the Texas Centennial Celebration he convinced the editor of *Vogue* magazine to come to Texas. Even though the woman had never been farther west than the Hudson River, Stanley kidnapped, er, went to New York City and accompanied her back to Dallas on the train. After days and days of Stanley Marcus using all the wily sale tricks he learned huckstering for the *Saturday Evening Post*, the woman didn't stand a chance. By the time she was back in New York, she proclaimed fashion lived in the Wild West, and Texas became more than just a state but a bigger than life land that made the rest of the country curious to learn more. *Fortune* Magazine called the city Dallas in Wonderland.

Personal service remained the most important part of the Neiman-Marcus success story. Stanley reportedly told sales people to treat everyone who walked in the door like a millionaire, even the ones in dirty, ratty clothes. There were so many oil fortunes being made in Texas in the 50s, 60s, and 70s, that many customers who looked like hobos who just jumped off a train were oilmen who either just struck it rich, or might the next day.

Stanley loved Christmas, as do all retailers, but no one else created exorbitant His and Her Fantasy gifts that got more media play than Hollywood gossip. The first was a live Black Angus bull that came with a sterling silver barbecue cart for $1,925 (in 1952, when that was a year's pay for many people). How about His and Her mummy cases for $16,000 in 1971? Autographed letters from George and Martha Washington for $8,500 in 1976? His and Hers robots in 2003, for $400,000?

Such skillful media manipulation, along with and expanding base, made Neiman-Marcus famous in popular culture as well as shorthand for high quality and high dollar. Even the famous Neiman-Marcus $250 Cookie Recipe story is expensive. A cookie recipe for $250? Of course it's nonsense (Neiman-Marcus always gave away recipes to customer who asked, and didn't even sell chocolate chip cookies when the story started), and you can download the recipe yourself from the store website.

The really funny part of all this? Stanley Marcus loved collecting rare books so much he almost started a business brokering same when he left college. His father talked him into coming back to the family business by telling him his store salary would allow him to build his rare book collection that much faster.

There you go: the man who may be the most famous retailer ever took the job just to feed his book addiction. That makes the Texas Hysterical Society Honchos and Honchettes all the more proud of native son Stanley Marcus.

> *During the middle 1980s, the Texas Hysterical Society Head Honcho, a violinist, played for a party at the Adolphus Hotel for the Queen of Siam (back when it was still Siam). Stanley Marcus was one of the hosts. The sight of Stanley Marcus and the Queen of Siam and the rest of the guests doing some sort of far eastern conga line remains a cherished, but hard to explain, memory.*

## Need a Toothpick?

Another natural resource abundant in Texas is lumber. Well, technically, lots and lots of trees (mostly pine) that can be turned into lumber. The first sawmills in Texas predate the Texas Revolution by a couple of decades. The first steam sawmill in Texas started up in 1829, but that pesky Santa Anna destroyed it in 1836. After Texas became independent from Mexico, sawmills popped up all over the Gulf Coast to provide building materials for the flood of New Texans arriving post haste. Hope that was legal immigration.

East Texas became the focus of the lumber companies after the Civil War, and the years between 1880 to the Great

Depression were the lumber equivalent of oil well gushers. The pine forest covered all or most of 48 counties with trees as tall as 150 feet and five feet in diameter. 1880 started the boom, because that was about the time the railroads made their way to Texas and could ship cut lumber back east economically.

The high point of lumber production in Texas was in 1907: 2.25 billion (with a B) board feet, the most before or since. Texas native John Henry Kirby (born in Tyler County in 1860) became known as the Prince of the Pines after rolling up 14 different sawmills into the Kirby Lumber Company in 1901. A well-rounded entrepreneur, Kirby bought the timber, mineral, and surface rights to nearly a million acres in Southeast Texas. An important name locally and nationally, Kirby also owned the Houston Oil Company.

> *The California crunch really is the result of not enough power-generating plants and then not enough power to power the power of generating plants.*
> *– George W. Bush, Honorary Texan*

The low point of lumber production in Texas was the horrible working conditions and deplorable treatment of those wielding saws and axes. Slavery was dead, but the lumber barons didn't get the news. If only the workers could have gotten on an early 20th century version of *Axe Men* on the History Channel, life might have been better for them. As it was, they made around $2 per day. Until the Texas legislature established the first version of a workman's compensation law and system, injured workers were at the mercy, or the lack of mercy, of the owners and managers. If that reminds you of how badly cowboys were paid and treated, thank your lucky stars you were born in a more enlightened era.

By the end of the Lumber Years, over 59 billion (with a B) board feet of lumber came from over 18 million acres of virgin pine. After the forests disappeared, so did the lumber barons,

51

and most of them headed to the Pacific Northwest to attack new virgin forests.

> *When confronted with a mountain to move, start with one rock.*
> *— Wanda Brice, CEO of the Women's Museum in Fair Park*

After the Depression, some smart folks (led by chemist Charles Holmes Herty) figured out a way to produce white newsprint from southern yellow pine trees. Thus became a second boom, followed later by another when the Southern Pine Lumber Company began making plywood from southern pines. By this time, lumber companies could use just about all parts of a pine tree to make things from boards to particle boards to fiber boards to wood flour, along with newsprint and other paper products.

As always happens, successful family businesses (sawmills) were acquired by the huge national chains, and the Texan flavor of the Texas lumber business changed for the worse. In the day, the lumber business was the largest employer of labor, the largest manufacturing business, and, oh yes, produced the most income, of any other Texas industry. Remember those good old days (if you were a lumber baron, not a worker) next time you grab a toothpick to pry some steak from between your teeth.

## Red Adair

Born Paul Neal Adair in Houston on June 18, 1915, Red Adair became famous for his ability to snuff out the worst types of fires: flaming oil and gas wells. His exploits putting out the Devil's Cigarette Lighter, a gas field fire in the Sahara in 1962, became the basis of the movie *Hellfighters* starring John Wayne. Having John Wayne play you in a movie is a pretty big honor, even for a Texan.

He learned his firefighting techniques in the Army and working for the M. M. Kinley Company. Drafted in 1945 (getting drafted at age 30 at the end of the war could be considered bad luck but it certainly worked out for him), Adair was assigned to the 139th Bomb Disposal Squadron in Japan. There he learned about controlling explosives and explosions.

That knowledge, combined with what he learned from Myron Kinley, allowed him to prosper in a small, rarefied, and extremely dangerous field. He started his own company in 1959, the Red Adair Company, and outfitted his workers in bright red uniforms in a brilliant bit of marketing. The main technique he used was a controlled explosion that blew all the oxygen away from the fire, snuffing out the flame.

After the Persian Gulf War ended in 1991, Adair was hired to put out oil and gas wells set ablaze by Saddam Hussein's retreating troops. Experts estimated it would take three to five years to put them all out. The Red Adair Company finished all 117 in nine months.

> *If you think it's expensive to hire a professional to do the job, wait until you hire an amateur.*
> *– Red Adair, www.redadair.com*

Adair became well known to the world at large, which happens when John Wayne plays you in a movie. People often told the joke about a Texan dying and meeting the Devil (obviously a joke, if a Texan doesn't go to heaven). As the Devil showed him around Hell, he remarked, "Have you ever seen a fire that big?"

"Nope," replied the fictional Texan. "But we got a boy from Houston who can put that out for you."

Red was quoted one time that he'd made a deal with the Devil, who promised him an air-conditioned spot in Hell. Why? So Red wouldn't put those fires out. Guess Red heard those jokes, too.

The only regret from the Texas Hysterical Society about Red Adair? No one thought to hire him to quench something bigger than Hell's fires: politician's greed.

> *In 1894, when the City of Corsicana (southeast of Dallas) drilled for water, they struck oil instead. Annoyed, they bypassed the oil and drilled deeper until they found artesian water.*

## *You Pays Yer Money and You Takes Yer Chances*

Ann Richards, when governor, pushed to get the Texas Lottery approved, and in fact bought the first ticket in June of 1992 (she didn't win). By late 1993, Texas Lottery sales took over the lead spot from Florida. When the Texas Lottery Commission was legislated into existence in 1993 to take over the reins from the Texas Comptroller of Public Accounts, they also took over control of charitable bingo games from the Texas Alcoholic Beverage Commission. How the TABC was in charge of bingo games is a mystery that no doubt ends in a meeting between a lobbyist bearing gifts and a greedy politician. If someone knows, please tell us.

In the beginning, all Lottery proceeds went into the General Revenue Fund, even though during the campaign to pass the Lottery, supporters only talked about how many millions of extra dollars would be available to fund education needs. Since 1997, all proceeds have gone to the Foundation School Fund and are applied directly to education, not general revenue needs. The Lottery Commission says over $17 billion (with a B) has been generated for the state since the Lottery began.

One should appreciate the irony of the Texas Lottery funding education, since the result of a good education should be a good job that precludes believing a Lottery ticket is the only way to fiscal salvation. As the bumper sticker says: *A*

*Lottery is a tax on people who are bad at math.* But funding education with Lottery money does make it clear that getting a great education in Texas public schools can be a real gamble (read the history of the Dallas Independent School District).

One would expect a good place to buy a Lottery ticket would be a casino, but that's not the case in Texas. Casino gambling has been banned in Texas pretty much forever. You can thank the lobbyists hired by the owners of casinos in Louisiana and Oklahoma for that bit of legislative duplicity. Lottery and horse racing, but not casinos? How does that make sense? Maybe the casinos should promise to help pay for education.

> *Poor is a way of life, and broke is just a temporary state.*
> *— Larry North, Honorary Texan*

Major sports franchises strongly discourage gambling on the outcomes of games, for the obvious worry that gambling money would corrupt the sports. This is the primary reason no major professional sport has a team in Nevada, where gambling is legal.

So how did the Texas Lottery convince the NFL to allow them to sell scratch off tickets with the Dallas Cowboys and Houston Texans on them? Can a person reconcile buying a Lottery ticket with a Cowboys star but not being able to bet on whether the Cowboys can beat the Texans?

State of Texas: No gambling (except the state run Lottery and horses, and three greyhound dog tracks), or casinos, because casinos would endorse gambling, er, endorse bad gambling.

NFL: No gambling except for Lottery scratch off tickets, because we're serious about no gambling. Really, we're serious. But scratch offs are just so darn cute we couldn't say no. We have no idea what you mean by the term "gateway drug."

# Law
# and
# Politics

## *The Chicken Ranch*

Yes, this is the place made famous by the musical and later movie *The Best Little Whorehouse in Texas*, and the ZZ Top hit "La Grange." There's more story here (130 years' worth) than most people know, so let's skip the foreplay and get to it.

Way back in 1844, during the Republic of Texas days, a widow named "Mrs. Swine" (sounds like an alias) arrived from New Orleans with three young women, all in a wagon. The story from the time said locals called the women "piglets" because of Mrs. Swine's name and the fact none of them were exactly, um, gorgeous. One was named Tillie but there are no records of the names of the other two. All four took up residence near the saloon in a friendly hotel, where introductions were made in the lobby, business was transacted with Mrs. Swine, and services rendered upstairs.

Mrs. Swine followed the smart tradition of madams everywhere and made friends with the local constabulary and donated money to local charities. It's harder for the local citizenry to become morally outraged about prostitution if they know, and receive money from, those involved.

> *Never see a lawyer without seeing a lawyer first.*
> *– Craig Hall, Honorary Texan*

But politics intervened during the Civil War, when Mrs. Swine and young Tillie were accused of being Yankee traitors and run out of town. Since New Orleans, where they came from, was as southern as La Grange, perhaps competitors fanned the flames of Yankee outrage.

After Mrs. Swine and Tillie disappeared, respectable houses (the judgment of the times) were lacking in La Grange. Saloons took up the slack but without the gentility and professionalism shown by Mrs. Swine. But La Grange remained a destination spot for prostitution, with a red light district moved from the saloons in town out to the banks of the Colorado River.

Respectability returned when Miss Jessie Williams (originally named Faye Stewart) arrived from Waco in 1905. Following the pattern established by Mrs. Swine, Miss Jessie became a good corporate citizen and made friends with local law enforcement, probably really good friends (wink-wink, nudge-nudge). Warned by her good legal friends, Miss Jessie closed the house in town before a crackdown, and bought eleven acres with two buildings outside the city limits of La Grange on the road to Houston. Thus began the real "Chicken Ranch" of Broadway and rock and roll fame.

Cleverly, Miss Jessie appointed two sisters to marketing positions in 1917. They spent time sending letters to local boys serving in World War I, promising a grand soldier's welcome for their little soldiers if they came to visit. And they did. More customers meant more girls, which meant more rooms built crazily on the original structures as needed and when needed.

The local sheriff, Will Lossein, visited the Chicken Ranch each evening, on official business. Really, official business (that's his story, and no surprise, he's sticking to it). He visited with Miss Jessie who passed along gossip and information told to the girls as pillow talk and during bragging sessions among clients. The sheriff closed almost all criminal cases in La Grange with this information, and the safety of Miss Jessie and her house was guaranteed.

> *As they say around the Texas Legislature, if you can't drink their whiskey, screw their women, take their money, and vote against 'em anyway, you don't belong in office.*
> *— Molly Ivins - Honorary Texan,*
> *famous writer on Texas politics*

During the Great Depression, times became tough even for love, or at least for lust. Lowered prices helped, but business still dwindled. Hungry girls created the need for a new payment system, announced on the sign as "One chicken for one screw." We expect chicken rustling became a major crime. The girls then had plenty of food and were happy once again, Miss Jessie even opened a side business selling poultry and eggs, and the Chicken Ranch got its name.

During World War II the same marketing approach based on pen pal wenches started up again, and business grew. Miss Jessie kept running the house even after being forced into a wheelchair by arthritis in the 1950s.

Enter Edna Milton (Miss Edna) who came from Oklahoma in 1952, took over managing the Chicken Ranch, and then bought it outright from Miss Jessie. Miss Edna added her own management style, based on Miss Jessie's formula that was based on Mrs. Swine's.

All the girls were checked by the doctor each week and shopped in town to strengthen local ties. Supplies for the house were bought from local merchants as well, and Miss Edna became one of the leading philanthropists in town.

T. J. Flournoy, the new sheriff elected in 1946, relied on the Chicken Ranch gossip to solve crimes just as his predecessor did. But modern technology allowed him to put a direct phone line from the Sheriff's office to Miss Edna, so he could get the news via phone. Sometimes technology really takes the fun out of a job, doesn't it? But the job he did he did well, and solved every murder and bank robbery in the area.

---

In the Old West, it was possible to die from five aces.

---

The Chicken Ranch flourished, although Miss Edna's self-imposed limit of 16 girls meant clients often lined up outside the door on busy nights, and most nights were busy. Between local military bases and Texas A&M, business was good. One military base even ran helicopter shuttles to and from the Chicken Ranch.

Business remained good for years and years, and the local town and Sheriff protected the Chicken Ranch and the traditions. But leave it to an outsider to mess things up, and one did. In mid-1977, Houston consumer affairs reporter Marvin Zindler ran a weeklong story on the ranch, alleging corruption and ties to organized crime. Turns out the state had already run a two-month surveillance of the Chicken Ranch and found no evidence of either. No mention was made why the Department of Public Safety couldn't find evidence of prostitution during their two-month investigation.

Dolph Briscoe, the governor at the time, was forced into action by the publicity and ordered the ranch closed (forcing Sheriff Flournoy do the dirty work). Although an institution (for 130 years) of fine reputation and local civic involvement, prostitution was (and still is) illegal in Texas (for sex, but not for politicians and lobbyists trading money for favors). Even after all the publicity about the closing, clients showed up with money in hand for more than two years.

Part of the original building was moved to Dallas in September 1977 and opened as a restaurant with the name the Chicken Ranch, selling mostly chicken dishes. Miss Edna was the hostess. Alas, the restaurant failed in January 1978 (faster than most restaurants die). It seems the appeal of the Chicken Ranch wasn't the chicken.

*Think Texas laws are friendly to politicians? Yes they are, because politicians write the laws. That explains how sitting U.S. Senator Lyndon Baines Johnson ran for re-election as Senator as well as vice president in 1960. Senator Lloyd Bentsen did the same in 1988.*

## More IRS Misdeeds

Texas has learned to admit mistakes and make amends, at least to citizens wrongly convicted and sent to prison. In 2009, the state Legislature raised the payment to "exonerees" from $50,000 to $80,000 per year, plus an annuity. That's the good news. And Texas is more generous than most states that provide payments, unlike the 23 states that just say "sorry" when they let the wrongly convicted out of prison. New Hampshire, for example, only pays a maximum of $20,000, no matter how many years of wrongful imprisonment are involved.

The bad news? Much of that "sorry for locking you up by mistake" money may get sucked up by the Infernal Revenue Service. Currently, the IRS considers payments to the wrongly imprisoned the same as lottery winnings, and therefore highly taxable.

Let's see – you win the lottery, and you pay some taxes. Understandable. You are wrongfully thrown in prison, finally get due process, and are released. The state of Texas pays you $80,000 per year in prison, which won't make up for being in prison, but at least is better more than a bus ticket. Then the IRS ogres swoop down and take a big chunk of your money.

Texas is far nicer than the IRS, and now we have proof. Even Texas on the hottest summer day is nicer than the IRS.

> *The Texas State Legislature meets for five months every two years. Why? The good people of the State of Texas can't stand any more help than that. Petitions appear now and then asking the Legislature to meet every three years, and thus improve the welfare of the citizens by 50 percent.*

## Divorce Will Find a Way... Someday

In the fall of 2009, the Texas Attorney General appealed a ruling from Dallas District Judge Tena Callahan stating she had jurisdiction to hear a suit for divorce. Why is this notable? Because the divorce petition was filed by one man against another.

At this writing, marriage in Texas is allowed between a man and woman only. Same sex marriages are illegal in Texas, as they are in about forty other states.

But if same sex marriage is illegal, does that mean same sex divorce is likewise banned? According to the Attorney General, allowing same sex divorce would also allow same sex marriage. The Texas Hysterical Society isn't sure that logic is properly applied. If it's against the law to injure someone, is it then against the law to heal them?

Many find this whole same sex marriage argument to be a bit tiresome. Why should same sex couples be spared the same misery, er, joy, shared by traditional couples in marriage?

Too bad. For now, if you're a married same sex couple and you move to Texas, you're stuck with each other.

## Fergusons, Meet the Fergusons

The first governor in the U.S. to be impeached was Jim Ferguson in 1917, known as "Farmer Jim" and husband to Miriam "Ma" Ferguson. People at the time shouldn't have been surprised. Farmer Jim was thrown out of school at age 12 for disobedience. Then he became a lawyer.

Miriam Amanda Wallace Ferguson (Ma), was the second woman governor elected in the U.S., missing the first spot by just 15 days to Nellie Ross in Wyoming, in November 1924. Running after her husband Farmer Jim was impeached, Ma promised "two governors for the price of one." She lost in 1926, but ran again in 1930 (and lost). She ran and won in 1932. At 65 years of age, she ran again in 1940, and while she lost, she received over 100,000 votes.

During her tenure, Ma passed a law banning the wearing of masks in public. Not as a slap to Halloween, but as an attack on the Ku Klux Klan. She said, "Let us take the sheets and put them back on the beds!"

> *The governor of a state needs to save money, and everybody knows a wife can always save two dollars where a husband can only save one.*
>
> *— Miriam 'Ma' Ferguson*

## The Smartest Crooks in the Room

Texas tries to be the biggest in everything, including, unfortunately, some of the bad things. In the early 1960s Billie Sol Estes hit the news (and the jails) for selling investments that weren't, shall we say, entirely legal. In fact, the cotton storage facilities he supposedly had held less than Estes' own ego (nothing could hold his ego, and nothing was what the storage facilities were). The theft through fraud of about $24 million was pretty big money for the time, and a big scandal when all unraveled. People close to Billie turned up dead from "suicide" (officially). 57 federal counts of fraud were filed.

No one can forget Enron, the Houston company that set new heights of scandal, chicanery, and hubris. Being friends with people in very high places helped Ken Lay lead the lambs to the financial slaughter. They cornered the market on a long list of illegalities leading to several dozen criminal charges and 19 guilty plea deals. Lay managed to die from "natural causes" after being convicted but before serving prison time. He was, of course, out on appeal as most rich criminals are, when he died while living in his Houston palace of a home.

> *The first rule of holes: when you're in one, stop digging.*
> *— Molly Ivins, Honorary Texan*

Believe it or not, some Texans are lamenting the good old days of Enron executives strutting around all manly and in charge. Guess some of those Enron apologists forgot about little details such as those strutting executives demanding employees put all their retirement in Enron stock so the execs could keep the stock price up as they sold their own shares as fast as possible. Sinking ships and rats come to mind.

One giant business reform triggered directly by Enron's trampling of the legal books was the passing of the Sarbanes-Oxley law. This demands that corporate bad guys keep careful notes when they're breaking the law to make it easier for prosecutors later. So far, the law commonly called SOX has helped catch, let's see, no one. Seems most of the corporate bad guys aren't stupid enough to write down their illegal doings, which makes them smarter than the politicians who passed the law.

They certainly didn't catch R. Allen Stanford, head of the Houston-based Stanford Financial Group. Well, the offices were officially in Houston, but it seems all the money was in Antigua, a country with no extradition treaty to the U.S. but many banks filled with friendly bankers. Stanford was such a good customer of said banks the government of Antigua knighted him. Yes, a knighthood for hiding about $7 billion in Ponzi scheme money bilked from thousands of investors the world over. Stanford now serving 110 years in Florida prison.

Stanford, born in Mexia and knighted in a Caribbean country known for laundering and hiding money, is Texas' leading financial criminal (at least so far). The trial has been concluded, and it went the one expects when your Chief Financial Officer makes a deal with the Feds. Stanford felt the noose tightening around his neck (metaphorically speaking, unfortunately).

In Ponzi schemes, in spite of Standford's best efforts, Texas comes in second to New York City and Bernie Madoff. His $60 Billion (or so) Ponzi scheme set the bar pretty high for Texas's criminals, but there are those out there determined to beat him. Let's just hope that SOX law catches them quickly. The Texas Hysterical Society doesn't mind Texas not coming in first in illegal categories.

Our criminals tend to be more bigger than life (Bonnie and

Clyde) than bigger than all the other worst criminals in US history.

## Helpful Police

Yes, times have been tough and public spending has been cut, but perhaps police training is one area that should be considered important. Or at least police training in Corpus Christi.

The Corpus Christi police, responding in 2009 to a report from an "unnamed youth," descended on a city park and carefully uprooted, bagged, and tagged 400 marijuana plants. Who would have the courage, or stupidity, to plant Weed in a public park?

Apparently no one, so the police get the FAIL label (from FailBlog.org). Turns out the "Weed" was "weed" in the form of Horse Mint. Being a member of the mint family, one might expect the minty freshness of the marijuana might have alerted at least one of the police officers to check more carefully, but no such luck.

On the other hand, the parked looked "real purty" when the police were done. And the local TV stations had a good time, which is always important.

---

*And now, will y'all stand and up be recognized?*
*– House Speaker Gib Lewis (to a group of observers in the*
*gallery, all of whom were sitting in wheelchairs.)*

---

## Police Humor. Really. It Happens Sometimes.

The good people of El Paso in 2009 heard the police chief, the no-nonsense Chief Greg Allen, propose an interesting way to deal with motorists caught using their cell phones while driving. Anyone talking and driving would have their phone confiscated and stomped to death by the police officer (the phone, not the driver). Chief Allen even made the point that since many officers wore boots, said boots would come in handy for phone stomping.

Announced on a morning TV show, the video soon hit YouTube and Facebook. Folks with phones and cars got a bit nervous, according to all accounts. Folks who hate people who yack and drive (erratically and dangerously) cheered.

Then, unfortunately, the anti-phone fans groaned as the word came out that the Chief was pulling a giant April Fool's prank on the citizens. No confiscation and no phone stomping.

We at the Texas Hysterical Society nominate Chief Allen for consideration of higher office. If he won't run for Governor, how about Highway Commissioner?

> *In Texas, a good friend will bail you out of jail. A great friend won't ask you what you did until you volunteer that information. And your best friend will be in the jail cell with you, saying, "hot damn that was fun!"*
>
> *– The Old Cowboy*

The Sheriff pulled up next to a pickup on the side of the road. Trash was flying out of the pickup bed over into the ditch.

"Bobby Joe, what the hell are you doing?" yelled the Sheriff. 'Can't you read that sign above your head?"

"Of course, I ain't dumb. I'm here because of that sign."

"What?"

"Read the sign Sheriff, read the sign. It says 'Fine for Dumping Garbage.'"

## Praise from Clyde

Clyde Barrow, the leader of the Bonnie and Clyde team of daring criminals that made bad news but good movies, loved to steal Ford cars for getaway vehicles. Here's the letter of appreciation he wrote the Ford company in 1934.

> Dear Sir,
> While I still have got breath in my lungs I will tell you what a dandy car you make. I have drove Fords exclusively when I could get away with one. For sustained speed and freedom from trouble the Ford has got ever other car skinned and even if my business hasent been strictkly legal it don't hurt enything to tell you what a fine car you got in the V-8. [sic]

Perhaps Clyde should have paid more attention in school. And, by the way, not robbed all those banks and shot all those people, too. It appears the laws of grammar were far down the list of laws broken by Bonnie and Clyde.

## More Helpful Lawyers

Isn't it nice to know Texas lawyers are looking out for the institution of marriage? Early in January 2010, family law attorney Brad LaMorgese from the Dallas office of McCurley Orsinger McCurley Nelson & Downing sent out a press release detailing how the post-holiday time bubbles over with divorces.

"People make it through the pressures of the holidays, then decide that they don't want to face those same arguments or disappointments again," said LaMorgese. Seems a little sad to think failing to keep your New Year's Resolution could lead to divorce, but that could happen. Once the disappointments start, they keep coming.

Of course, there's always more to the story. "There are greater opportunities for conflicts involving finances or relatives this time of year, plus it's also a time when it's normal to think about and make plans for the future," said LaMorgese. Those big Christmas parties full of your spouse's relatives can certainly be trying. Just thinking of all that time spent searching for the perfect gift for her sister-in-law, only to get a beaded ceiling fan pull that looked like it was made by a teenager during crafts time in summer camp, gets Your Humble Head Honcho's wife is laughing all over again.

People stick together for appearances at business and family parties, then vamoose. Guess they don't want to face those parties alone, or are afraid the spiked eggnog will be too tempting if they're single. On the other hand, stupidities after spiked eggnog have led to their own share of divorces.

Gentlemen, if you don't use at least half your brain to buy a nice gift for your wife, she may use her lawyer to get half of your worldly goods. The fanciest gift in town is cheaper than a divorce. And if you forget, the friendly lawyers will send out more press releases for your wife.

> *Never try to reason with an idiot. He'll drag you down to his level and beat you with experience. Some people apply the same advice to Yankees – don't argue with them, because they don't make any sense. Just say something they don't understand, like "bless your heart," and walk away.*
> *– The Old Cowboy*

Montgomery County decided to go all a'Twitter in 2009 on those caught drunk driving during the holidays, like Christmas, New Year's Eve, Memorial Day, and July 4th. All those arrested will be announced via Twitter, the micro-blogging service that limits posts to a total of 140 characters. Check out District Attorney Brett Ligon's Twitter page (http://twitter.com/MontgomeryTXDAO) to see if you know anyone.

Question: if too many need to be Twittered, will that keep the DA from getting ready to convict them?

### Remember the Alamo

"Remember the Alamo. It means: Don't get mad. Get

even."

How about that quote from Charles Terrell in a *Dallas Morning News* article back on January 3rd, 2010. Isn't that an interesting quote for someone in the criminal justice system? Especially since Terrell is the Texas Criminal Justice System Chairman, or was at the time of the quote.

> *To POLITICIANS we say, remain where you are; we have no room for you.*
>
> *— Jacob de Cordova, 1858*
>
> *PS: We still don't need any extra — the ones we have are more than we can stand. Hmm, that might not stop them. Hey, politicians: the ones here already stole everything, so there's nothing left for you.*

Eye for an eye, anyone? Any doubts now why native son comedian Ron White tells a great story about how other states are doing away with the death penalty, but Texas is putting in an express lane? That's his excellent analogy for expedited executions for certain crimes, a law that passed in Texas a few years ago.

> *A friend will help you move. A good friend will bring his own pickup. A really good friend will help you move a body.*
>
> *— The Old Cowboy*

## Box 13

This was the famous box stuffed with "interesting" votes in the 1948 runoff for U. S. Senate. Lyndon B. Johnson, running against former governor Coke R. Stevenson, was behind at the end of vote counting by 114 votes. Six days later, the Jim Wells County precinct managers happened to discover Box 13. Inside were 202 more votes for Johnson, and one for Stevenson. That type of total always eliminates suspicion, right? Throw the other team one vote?

Before modern PC outrage strikes, a little history. Johnson took it in the shorts in 1941 when the ballot stuffing went the other way, and he lost the primary in the Senate race to Pappy O'Daniel. He lost by 1,311 votes in 1941. In 1948, he won by 87. Those who say all the votes in Box 13 had the same handwriting and listed dead people just don't understand the world of 1940s Texas politics.

Over a million votes were cast, and Johnson won by 87. He also won a nickname, "Landslide Lyndon." After he became more powerful, few had the courage to use that nickname when he was within earshot.

## Cactus Jack (not the Serbian rock band)

What is it about the name "Cactus Jack" that entices musical bands so strongly? Could they all be honoring John Nance Garner, aka Cactus Jack, the first Texan to be vice president of the United States? Why would a Serbian rock band and an English country band both name themselves Cactus Jack? And how many other vice presidents get that kind of musical adulation? Are the Joe Biden's playing near you?

John Nance Garner, the thirty-second vice president of the U.S., was born in Detroit. No, not that one, the one in Red River County in East Texas. Officially John Nance Garner IV, he was the offspring of John Nance Garner III and wife Sarah Jane Guest Garner, who welcomed the Cactus Jack to-be on November 22, 1868. After Jack, they welcomed another dozen children. *Whew*.

Young Cactus escaped the Piney Woods of East Texas and attended Vanderbilt University in Nashville, Tennessee at age eighteen. The pull of the Piney Woods is strong, or Jack got ill (does homesickness for Texas count as an official illness?) and came home after one semester.

While such an abortive college career might doom a normal young man to a life of non-letters, Jack studied the law

71

on his own and passed the State Bar Exam in 1890. In those days, if you could pass the Bar, you got your lawyer label. Today you must go through law school to accumulate the proper amount of student debt, then take the Bar exam, before you can be a lawyer. Cactus Jack is an example of sheer talent beating out the traditional mashing of initiative, the hallmark of most schools.

> *The reason I believe in a large tax cut is because it's what I believe.*
> *— George W. Bush, Honorary Texan*

Lawyering took Cactus Jack to being the county judge in Uvalde County, far south from the shady East Texas pine trees. In 1893 his opponent for County Judge was Mariette Rheiner. To make up for defeating her, he married her two years later.

Moving up, Cactus Jack was in the Texas House of Representatives from 1898 to 1902. During that time, he earned his nickname by supporting the prickly pear cactus for State Flower rather than the eventual winner, the bluebonnet. That earned him the nickname of Cactus Jack.

Rebounding from such a defeat was tough, but Cactus Jack managed to move on up yet again to the U. S. House of Representatives in 1902. He represented a brand new district that was tens of thousands of acres of empty rural South Texas. Evidently, he taught his namesake cactus plants to vote, because he was elected fourteen more times, until 1933. He moved up yet again to be the Speaker of the House of Representatives in 1931.

> *It's an honor to be the first woman of the Supreme Court, but it will be even better when we get the second cowgirl on the Supreme Court.*
> *— Sandra Day O'Connor*

One of the reasons he may have gotten so many Speaker votes was his popular evening "board of education" meetings during Prohibition. To "strike a blow for liberty," Cactus Jack served alcohol. Politicians being politicians, Cactus Jack must have had a big bunch of fellow board members.

To repay their debts for his "liberty" parties, his friendly politician buddies convinced him to run for President in 1932. Franklin Roosevelt eventually got the lead, but couldn't get enough delegates at the Democratic convention to become the clear winner. Cactus Jack offered his delegates for the job of vice president, and the duo won the nomination, then the White House.

Figuring he would be the natural choice to carry on Roosevelt's policies, Cactus geared up to run at the end of Roosevelt's second term. After all, the other Presidents followed the (then) unwritten rule and bowed out after two terms. Not Eleanor's husband; he wanted more. Cactus continued his campaign, but lost. He then let his disappointment in how Roosevelt's New Deal policies treated the Democratic platform go public, and became a detractor after he'd spent the eight previous years shaping many New Deal policies and projects.

Was Cactus tough? He must have been, because John L. Lewis, the big dog labor leader, called him "a labor-baiting, poker-playing, whiskey-drinking, evil old man." High praise from Lewis.

> The Texas Legislature passed a law in 2007 guaranteeing that no Texan's Bible could be seized "for the satisfaction of debts."

On November 22, 1963, President John F. Kennedy called from Fort Worth to wish Cactus Jack a happy birthday. Nice homage to an "evil old man," and true Texan. Too bad Kennedy couldn't call him for his next birthday.

Cactus Jack died on November 7, 1967, at the age of 98 years and 350 days. So far, he holds the record for longest living vice president.

Most people know Cactus Jack from his famous quote saying the job of vice president "isn't worth a bucket of warm spit." As with many famous quotes, this one is also wrong. Cactus Jack said the job wasn't worth "a bucket of warm piss." He also called writers who used the "politically correct" version pantywaists. Somehow, we think Cactus Jack Garner might have called them something much more earthy.

Honestly, though, wouldn't Cactus Jack and the Buckets be a great name for a country band?

## *Failure to Yield*

Col. Edward Green bought the first car delivered in Texas in 1899. Built in St. Louis, the car was delivered to Col. Green by the designer so he could train the good Colonel in driving and maintenance.

Green lived in Terrell, but kept his mistress in Dallas so as not to upset the good people of Terrell (we're guessing that also kept Mrs. Col. Green in the dark). Since everyone wants to take their new car on a road trip, Green and the designer decided a trip to see the other woman was a great idea. Off they went.

Things were going wonderfully at first, since there were no red lights or stop signs to slow them down. That is until they hit Forney, a small town about halfway between Terrell and Dallas. The lack of stop signs and traffic lights meant the driver of a horse drawn wagon felt he had the same right of way as Col. Green (even though neither of them really knew about the rules for right of way).

You guessed it: the first car in Texas, on the first road trip, bounced off a wagon and landed in a ditch. A Forney blacksmith had to repair the car (and tried to cheat the insurance company by using wagon parts rather than official car parts). Since love, or at least lust, can't be denied, the repaired car soon got back on the road.

> My faith in the Constitution is whole; it is complete; it is total. I am not going to sit here and be an idle spectator to the diminution, the subversion, the destruction of the Constitution.
>
> – Barbara Jordan, Congresswoman
> During the 1974 Watergate impeachment hearings

## When Santa Took Rather Than Gave

Two days before Christmas in the year 1927, Santa Claus sauntered down the streets of a small town in central Texas named Cisco. Children smiled and waved, and Santa waved back, at least until he got to the First National Bank of Cisco. Then he became decidedly less jolly.

Marshall Ratliff, inside the Santa suit, had just gotten out of prison for robbing a bank in Valera, Texas. He and his brother Lee planned to rob the bank in Cisco together, but Lee once again became the guest of the state in a crossbar hotel. So Marshall rounded up a couple of buddies. He wore the Santa costume to hide his identity because he'd lived in Cisco and had previously been arrested by the Chief of Police, G. E. Bedford. No one recognized him at first, including the children who followed him into the bank.

> I'd just make a little bit of money. I wouldn't make a whole lot.
>
> – House Speaker Gib Lewis
> (discussing how he would benefit from a bill he introduced)

When one accomplice started waving his gun around, Santa, or rather Ratliff, jumped around the counter and started filling his toy sack with greenback toys from the cash drawers.

Ratliff and his three buddies kept an eye on everyone and grabbed all the dough they could.

They didn't, unfortunately for them, keep an eye on one Mrs. B. P. Blassengame and her six-year-old daughter, Frances. The mother and daughter followed Santa into the bank so Frances could say hello.

Mrs. Blassengame realized what was up, pushed her way through the customers and bad guys, and pushed Frances out the back door. "Santa" and his co-conspirators yelled at her and threatened to shoot, but Mrs. Blassengame followed Frances out the back way and ran to the police station. Guess who was in the police station? Ratliff's old friend Chief Bedford.

There was a gunfight in the alley, where Chief Bedford was mortally wounded. There was a gunfight in the street in front of the bank, where over 100 shots were fired back and forth.

Remember, this was Texas in 1927. Many folks carried guns. Folks who didn't have their guns ran to the hardware store to buy guns and ammo real fast so they could join in the fracas.

Adding more fuel to the flaming fracas, the Texas Bankers Association had recently offered a $5,000 reward for any bank robber, as long as the robber was dead. And $5,000 was a big heaping pile of money in 1927.

Ratliff in his Santa suit and his three cohorts grabbed hostages, used them for shields, and jumped in their getaway car. Unfortunately, perhaps because they were auditioning for a part in *Stupid Criminals of 1927, The Movie*, they had forgotten to get gas and started looking for another car before they got out of town.

They carjacked an Oldsmobile driven by a 14-year-old boy name Woodrow Wilson Harris. Shooting back at the mob from town growing closer each minute, the crooks transferred all their loot and hostages to the Oldsmobile, and then realized young Harris had taken the keys with him when he ran out of

76

the car. Pretty smart for a 14-year-old.

Jumping back into their own car, with the hostages, the crooks left one of their own men behind as he was too badly wounded to continue. Again, auditioning for *Stupid Criminals*, they left the money behind as well. $12,400 in cash and $150,000 in non-negotiable securities were grabbed by the townspeople and returned to the bank.

> *The American Dream is not dead. It is gasping for breath, but it is not dead.*
>
> *– Barbara Jordan*

Ratliff and the remaining crooks, weak from wounds and lack of food, were captured during a shootout the next day. Ratliff had six pistols stuck in his Santa suit, with an equal number of bullet holes through said suit (but he lived). Seven days after the robbery, the last two crooks were captured. Wounded and worn out, they gave up without a fight.

Convicted for armed robbery on January 27, 1928, Ratliff, nee Santa, was scheduled for execution on March 30. Ratliff appealed, and started acting crazy to try and create an insanity plea. The good folks of Eastland County, where Cisco and the bank robbery were, petitioned to get him back in their custody when they found out he hadn't been executed.

Ratliff actually convinced two jailers he was paralyzed to the point they started feeding and bathing him, and even taking him to the toilet. This worked until he grabbed a pistol from one guard, fatally wounded the other, and tried to escape. Unfortunately for Ratliff, the other guard, Pack Kilbourn, was tougher. Townspeople watched from beyond the locked jail doors as Kilbourn beat Ratliff unconscious, then threw him back in his cell.

Now that everyone in town knew Ratliff wasn't crazy, or at least not crazy in the clinical, "get out of jail" sense, they took action. The next morning, they pulled him out of jail and took him to a vacant lot. Ironically, the lot was behind a theater hosting a play named "The Noose." Taking the name to heart, the mob strung up Ratliff. The town later put a marker on the pole that supported the noose.

No one from the mob was ever indicted for the lynching. After all, in Texas, a common defense in the Old West days was, "he needed killing." Ratliff certainly did, and thus ended the biggest manhunt in the history of Western Texas.

Although the First National Bank of Cisco has moved to a new building, you can see the story of Santa Claus Robbery in a painting there. You can also read clippings and stories from back in the day. The Texas Historical Commission put a plaque in the bank marking the robbery as a true Texas-sized historical event.

## *Open Season On Bank Robbers*

Normally, we think of bankers as rather staid, conservative folks and real pillars of the community. After the financial meltdown and watching the banks get billions of dollars from Uncle Sam and still paying themselves millions in bonuses, the reputation of bankers has taken a serious nosedive.

But no recent bank group has done anything as despicable as the Texas Banking Association did in 1926. They established the Dead Bank Robber Reward Program. There had been so many bank robberies (3-4 per day in Texas) that drastic measures were needed, and the bankers took drastic steps. The bounty on bank robbers was $5,000 cash.

> *My friend, I can explain it to you, but I can't understand it for you.*
> *— Comptroller John Sharp*

You read the title of the program correctly: Dead Bank Robber. The bankers weren't interested in seeing bank robbers caught and sentenced to three squares a day in a square cell; they wanted them blown away at the time of the crime. That's why most of the town of Cisco grabbed their guns and chased after the Santa Claus bank robbers at Christmas time in 1927.

As one might reasonably expect, things got out of hand quickly. Suckers were hired to rob a bank, then shot by those hiring them for the reward. People who looked sorta kinda like a bank robber were shot, often by people who had other issues with the now-dead supposed bank robber. Local law enforcement officers sometimes duped criminals into a robbery followed by an ambush, so the officers could split the reward.

Since the Texas Banking Association wasn't really as hard hearted and cold blooded as the program made them seem, they amended the program. They specified that only "legally killed bank robbers" could be turned in for the reward. There, is that clear now? Fire away, but legally.

Did it slow down bank robberies? Nope. Nothing slowed down crime in general through the Great Crime Wave of 1933-34. Bank robberies did slow down after the federal government started guaranteeing bank deposits and made bank robbery a federal crime, investigated by the FBI.

> *It was not so much a matter of me being desperate for money as it was just being real damn mad at banks and bankers.*
> *– Lawrence Pope, bank robber, 1960*
> *PS: Most Texans are still damn mad at banks and bankers.*

Believe it or not, the reward program stayed active until 1964, even though law enforcement officials strongly objected. Too bad they quit the program before 2008. Could be, many of the bank and financial services executives who stole the billions missing from our 401k programs could be considered bank robbers. The $5,000 wouldn't be enough to recover the homes the bankers gleefully foreclosed on, but it sure would make some people feel better to go bank robber hunting once again.

## Henry Smith the StarMan

Where did Texas get the star? Say hello to Henry Smith, a man born in Kentucky in 1788 and who arrived in Texas in 1827. Early on he taught school then caught the political bug. Before he knew it, in 1834, the Mexican governor of the Texas area named him an "outstanding citizen" and appointed him political head honcho of the Texas area.

As the first governor of the Texas region (still a Mexican province), Smith received some important papers in the first few days of his appointment. Needing a seal for the wax stamp that made things oh so official, Smith pulled a big brass button from his coat. Luckily the coat button had a five-pointed star rather than a Chanel or Louis Vuitton logo. A CC or LV on the Texas flag wouldn't look that good. Some accounts put the date of Smith and the Star in 1821, which was six years before he even got to Texas. Oops.

Little did the Mexican Powers That Be realize that Smith moved from Texas fever to independence fever. They might should have asked why he was fighting in the Battle of Velasco in 1832, where he was wounded pretty badly. But they didn't.

> The only things in the middle of the road are yellow stripes and dead armadillos.
>
> – Jim Hightower

Fighting the good fight from the inside, Smith became part of the war party, as opposed to the peace party. Smith proclaimed Texas was already an independent state and free of Mexico, which tended to aggravate the Mexican authorities who appointed him. Imagine how upset they were when they heard he had gotten some votes for President of Texas in 1836, even though he told voters he supported Sam Houston and begged them to do the same.

How about this for a bit of bizarre family history: Smith married three times, to women named Harriet, Elizabeth, and Sarah Gillett. Yes, sisters. Evidently, when you find a mother-in-law you like, you stick with her.

## Belle Plain

Those who found the Chicken Ranch too gentile and civilized may have preferred Belle Plain, a "town" of crude shacks built just over the Hutchinson county line from Borger in 1927. The Texas Rangers drove out a large number of prostitutes, bootleggers, and gamblers from Borger, and the expelled quickly threw together a town named Belle Plain just out of reach of the Hutchinson authorities. Belle Plain didn't "have" a red light district, it "was" a red light district.

Here's the lyrics from a popular folksong of the day:

*Let's sing a song of Belle Plain,*
*Famed for its graft and rot.*
*It's just a wide place on the road,*
*This town that God forgot.*
*For this village boasts of deeper sin,*
*Than Sodom ever knew,*
*Come lend an ear, kind stranger,*
*And I'll whisper them to you.*
*(By the wildly prolific composer, Anonymous)*

Forgive us for being cynical, but the consensus at the Grand Hall of the Texas Hysterical Society is that the song was written by the Belle Plain Chamber of Commerce to draw customers. This song probably drew more business than a series of billboards.

The time was 1927, the middle of Prohibition, hence the popularity of bootleggers. Belle Plain covered the gamut, with bootlegged beer and whiskey. But as fast as it grew, the various miscreants scattered, leaving a handful of buildings still in use in 1929. And after the repeal of Prohibition in 1933, what was left of Belle Plain disappeared as well.

> *If you're going to play the game properly you'd better know every rule.*
>
> *– Barbara Jordan*

## Hell's Half Acre in Fort Worth

Hell's Half Acre was a common name for various red light districts around Texas and beyond, which is odd because all were larger than a half acre. Perhaps our elders loved the alliteration and the chance to use a curse word.

The most famous Hell's Half Acre was in Fort Worth in the 1870s. Built as a rest stop for cattle drives heading north through Fort Worth, saloons and brothels and everything else catering to a lonely cowboy with money in his pocket appeared as soon as the first cowboy jingled two coins together. By the 1880s the area had grown to about 2.5 acres full of crime and violence to the point the few law enforcement attempts came to naught.

After all, most of that money floating around found its way to the rest of the town. As always, red-light districts didn't flourish catering just to outsiders. But the good folks of Fort Worth were concerned about immorality of brothels, gambling dens, and, gasp, dance halls.

But the violence finally did the area in. A well-known hideout for criminals as notorious as Sam Bass, the numbers of thieves and criminals and the resulting violence that peaked in 1889 finally became too much for the Fort Worthians.

By the early 1900s Hell's Half Acre had become a shadow of its evil self. By 1917 the area was shut down completely.

Surprisingly, the success of Sundance Square and the

Stockyards areas haven't created a demand to recreate Hell's Half Acre for the tourists. That could be a real draw for the state PTA convention.

### Red Light Districts in Texas Between 1870-1910
**Austin**: Guy Town
**Amarillo**: The Bowery
**Beaumont**: the Reservation
**Corpus Christi**: The Flats
**Dallas**: Frogtown and Boggy Bayou
**El Paso**: The Utah Street Reservation
**Fort Worth**: Hell's Half Acre
**Galveston**: Postoffice Street (or Post Office District)
**Houston**: Happy Hollow
**San Antonio**: The Sporting District, or The District
**Waco**: Two Street

These were always located close to the downtown business district and the railroad depot. Adult entertainment venues included saloons, gambling clubs, and brothels. Dance halls and theaters, although not typically as illegal as the rest, tended to wind up these areas since that's where the tourists were.

> *On days when we rode on the roundups we were happy if we could stop for three drinks of water during the long day, and ecstatic if we could also have lunch along the way. Sometimes there was no time for either a drink of water or lunch. The job had to be done while there was daylight to see what we were doing.*
>
> *– Sandra Day O'Connor*

Waco has the distinction of being the first city to legislate the "red light district" in 1889. Well, they required Houses of Ill Repute to be in a particular area of the city, and charged fees based on the number of rooms in the houses and the number of women working there. Other red light districts were around already, of course, but Waco was the first to make the practice of official bribery via fees to allow illegal activities as officially legal.

## San Antonio's Sporting District

One might think this refers to the area around the wonderful Alamo Dome, but we're talking a different sport here. Just as Fort Worth had Hell's Half Acre, and Galveston had, well, Galveston through the 1920s to 1950s, San Antonio had the Sporting District.

Actually, we can credit San Antonio for the earliest recorded mention of prostitution in Texas history: 1817. Nine prostitutes made the news as they were expelled from San Antonio (look for the Fox News video of the perp walk on YouTube). Well, not yet San Antonio but San Fernando de Bexar, since Texas was still a Spanish province. And since San Antonio was one of the very first cities to become large enough to mention in Texas, one shouldn't be surprised they had the first mention of ladies with cash registers in place of their, er, morals.

But the Sporting District, sometimes called just The District, was one of the few organized by the city officials to contain and regulate prostitution, gambling, and other activities of the seedy urban underbelly, like bingo parlors.

Mayor Bryan Callaghan, often referred to as "King Bryan," decided since prostitution had always been a problem in a frontier society with few available women, the city should make some money therefrom. Starting in 1889, at King Bryan's decree, a special district was set aside for adult entertainment of all kinds, each requiring a city license ($500 annually per brothel). By the early 1900s the fees totaled around $50,000 annually, and the area was the largest in the state and ranked as high as third largest in the nation.

> *I seldom think about politics more than 18 hours a day.*
> — *Lyndon Baines Johnson*

Remember the "Blue Book" notebooks used during college for tests and other work? That's in interesting name choice, because San Antonio had *The Blue Book for Visitors, Tourists, and Those Seeking a Good Time While in San Antonio, Texas* way back in 1911. Guess the alliteration of blue and book just can't be beat.

Why did the Sporting District need a guidebook? Because it had gotten so large, over 10 square blocks, that it was easy to miss the best attractions (sort of like your typical guidebook at Disneyland but leading you to saloons rather than the "It's A Small World" ride). There were 24 Class A brothels listed, where "entertainment" fees started at $5, 20 Class B locations ($2.50), and 61 Class C houses (pocket change).

Class A houses often included orchestras, no doubt to cover the sounds of the games of slap and tickle going on upstairs. Many houses included gambling, making them seem like modern Las Vegas hotels (without the prostitution, of course, since that's illegal in the city of Las Vegas). Several of the saloons advertised themselves as family resorts, again sort of like the 1990s when Las Vegas casinos tried that ploy as well. Again, prostitution is illegal in Las Vegas, although there are an amazing number of beautiful young masseuses who will visit your hotel room to provide an expensive massage.

What the Blue Book didn't advertise was the large number of criminals hiding in the Sporting District. If you were a criminal, such as Butch Cassidy and the Sundance Kid, or a member of the Dillinger Gang, where would you hide when in San Antonio? After all, criminals like orchestras, too.

And you thought people always went to San Antonio to see the River Walk and the Alamo.

## *Galveston Was Wilder Before Spring Break Crazies*

People today may consider spring break on Galveston (and just about every southern beach) the ultimate wild, lawless party filled with drunken college kids. Sorry, but at least for Galveston, modern spring break crazy is pretty darn tame compared to Galveston from the early 1900s to the mid-1950s. During that time, Galveston was home to a continuous wild lawless party filled with drunken citizens, endorsed by city and law enforcement officials, and controlled by organized crime.

Sometimes called the "Free State of Galveston," the frontier tolerance for prostitution and gambling carried on through the early 1900s as the city rebuilt itself after the hurricane in 1900 that, well, gave them a blank slate to build upon. Postoffice Street (or the Post Office District, depending) became the red-light district as most of the brothels were there.

Unlike other adult districts in Texas, Galveston suffered from more organized criminal gangs. Prohibition in 1920 just made the gangs stronger, since they had the manpower and will to flaunt all manner of laws, not just the ones about drinking.

> *I believe in practicing prudence at least one every two or three years.*
> *– Molly Ivins, Honorary Texan*

In the mid-1920s Sam and Rosario Maceo, brothers, won the bad guy beauty pageant. Evidently they had great talent with violence and looked divine in the evening gown competition. Leveraging Galveston's ports to bring in liquor for Texas and much of the Midwest, income from liquor provided financing to expand gambling throughout the city. Most of the prostitution stayed on Postoffice Street, however. Fancy clubs with casinos brought in major entertainers from around the country. Tourism boomed, and local citizens and law enforcement variously endured and enjoyed the Free State of Galveston (free from vice laws, at least).

Mayor Herbert Yemon Cartwright, Jr., in office 1947 to 1955, was quoted in *Time* magazine saying the laws of Texas are violated in Galveston because Galvestonians think the laws are wrong. A committee researching the situation said, "That whether an activity is a 'vice' is a matter of purely personal philosophy; that a country that guarantees freedom of religion has no right to make laws about morals; that public opinion is divided as to whether smoking, drinking, gambling, and professional sex services are vices; that the church has the right to teach these certain acts are wrong, but has no right to prohibit them."

Ask any member of the business community at the time, and they would have agreed. The slogan used was that sin was good for business. Close down the house of gambling and prostitution and the tourists would stay home. Evidently, babes and Bingo were a bigger tourist draw than the beach.

Various morality crusaders and anti-prostitution groups started have a real impact nationally starting in the 1910s. By 1940 or so, most other "tourist attractions" of this sort were closed or strongly curtailed. But not in Galveston.

The mayoral election of 1955 would be a TV ratings blockbuster today. Cartwright felt regulated vice was the key to a well-run city. Challenger George Roy Clough (rhymes with rough) felt "clean but liberal" was the way to go. "Keep the chippies (juveniles) out of the place. Don't handle dope in any way, shape, or form. No showing of lewd sex movies." Above all, he said, reverse the damage down by do-gooders who closed the Post Office brothels and reopen the red light district.

Clough won, but the incumbent Police Commissioner also won. The reform-minded Police Commissioner candidate placed sixth in a field of six, in case you were wondering if the "clean and liberal" plan had coattails. But the Commissioner liked segregated vice and refused to reopen Post Office Street, saying, "the bawdyhouse district will never open again as long as I'm Police Commissioner."

Mayor Clough, the clean and liberal candidate, remember, declared, "In a resort town, prostitution is a biological necessity." And here's the quote of the day: "If God couldn't stop prostitution, why should I?" Can you imagine how much fun Fox News and MSNBC could have with quotes like this today? Where is Rush Limbaugh when you need him?

> *If God couldn't stop prostitution, why should I?*
> *– Galveston Mayor George Roy Clough*

But all things must come to an end, no matter how entertaining. Will Wilson, elected Texas State Attorney General, started pushing hard to clean things up in 1957, and made a big impact on prostitution in Galveston, Big Spring, Cuero, Texarkana, and Victoria. Beaumont and Port Arthur got swept clean in 1960. Only the Chicken Ranch flew the flag of law enforcement immunity.

Maybe the real reason Galveston cleaned up is that the Maceo brothers moved on to Las Vegas in the late 1940s. Legalized gambling must have been the lure, because we all know prostitution is illegal in Las Vegas. Just like it was in Galveston in the 1950s.

Two Yankees were driving through West Texas and let their speed get a bit out of control (easy to do on long, boring stretches of West Texas highway). Soon they noticed the flashing lights on the car of a state trooper.

When they finally pulled over, the driver rolled down his window and tried to look innocent when the trooper walked up with his nightstick. Without a word, the trooper smacked the driver in the head.

"Hey, why'd you hit me?" yelped the driver.

"You're in Texas, son. When you get pulled over, have

your license ready when the officer gets to the window."

"Sorry, sorry, we're just passing through. Here you go." The trooper took the license, went back to his car, and checked for any open tickets or warrants, but didn't find any.

The trooper gave the license back. "You're clean, and in the interest of promoting tourism and to give you a break since you're new here, I won't give you a ticket."

"You answered my wish, officer, thank you very much. I'll drive carefully now."

Without a word, the trooper went to the passenger side of the car and motioned for the man to roll down his window. When the man did, the trooper reached in and smacked him on the head with this nightstick.

"What was that for?" the passenger demanded.

"I'm just answering your wish, too," said the trooper.

"Huh?"

"About two miles down the road, you were going to say, 'I wish that guy would've tried that with me.'"

---

*I'm all ears.*
*– H. Ross Perot, during a Presidential debate*

---

A State Trooper pulled a car over on Interstate Highway 35 a few miles south of San Antonio. The driver had his window rolled down and his license at the ready, but he had done nothing wrong. In fact, he was getting a prize.

"Yes sir, that's right, you just won $5,000 from the state Safety Competition because everyone in the car is wearing their seat belts," said the trooper. "What do you think you'll do with the money?"

"You know," said the driver, "I think I'll go ahead and get my driver's license."

"Don't listen to him," said the woman in the passenger seat. "He gets all mouthy when he's drunk."

A man in the back seat woke up, saw the trooper, and

shook his head. "I knew we couldn't get far in a stolen car."

Just then the trooper heard a knock from the trunk. A muffled voice, in Spanish, asked, "Are we over the border yet?"

Subject: Sheriff's Exam in South Texas.

The sergeant sat in front of the candidate and put a service pistol on the table. "Your qualifications look great, but you need to take the Attitude Suitability Test now."

"Sure," said the recruit. "What do I need to do?"

"Take that weapon and go shoot six illegal aliens, six meth dealers, six Muslim extremists, six liberal Democrats, and a dentist."

"Why a dentist?" asked the recruit.

"That's the attitude we need here," said the sergeant. "Report for work on Monday."

> *If it's dangerous to talk to yourself, it's probably even dicier to listen.*
> *– Jim Hightower, Texas Agriculture Commissioner*

# **Sports**

## The Heisman Years at Rice

No Heisman Trophy winners have played for the Rice Owls, but John William Heisman coached there as their first full time football coach and athletic director from 1924 through 1927. Alas, in a Rice tradition to continue far too many times, Heisman posted a losing record. The best he did was his first year, 1924, when the team went 4-4. After going 2-6-1 in 1927, Houstonians ran Heisman out of town all the way back to New York City, where he became the athletics director of the Downtown Athletic Club of Manhattan.

In 1935, Heisman and the club started an award for the best football player east of the Mississippi. After Heisman's death in 1936, the club renamed the award the Heisman Memorial Trophy, and expanded the candidates to include all college football players in the country.

Heisman couldn't turn Rice into a national powerhouse, but he did end his career there and put Rice into the sports spotlight. Although Rice plays all the major collegiate sports, their contribution tends to be in the worlds of science and engineering.

> *The formula for success is simple: practice and concentration, then more practice and more concentration.*
> *– Babe Didrikson Zaharias*

## The Long Wave

Sure, you can surf in Texas. Galveston Island has good, well, usable waves. Many places along the Gulf of Mexico have decent reputations as surfing spots, even though Texas waves don't naturally rate high in the surfing community. But if you want a long, long, *long* wave, head to the Houston Ship Channel and tanker surf.

Only the hearty do this, because the Houston Ship Channel water is just as clean as you would expect for a dredged sewer ditch lined by oil refineries. But there are even charter companies now (like tankersurfcharters.com) that help you find the best tanker waves.

Surfers need a boat crew to take them out to deep water where the tankers run, and a local guide to help them avoid all the underwater hazards. Learning which ships are going which way takes some time as well. But people are doing this on a regular basis.

They don't get close enough to the tankers to cause ship captains any worry or put themselves in danger. Loaded tankers create enough of a wave for the surfers to ride happily two football fields away from the tankers.

The waves are only about knee high, useless for "real" surfers. But unlike surfing at a beach, where the ride ends when you hit the sand, you can go for miles surfing tanker waves. The long distance surf record now is seven miles on the Amazon River, but tanker surfers are working hard to break that record.

When a tanker surfer makes it eight or ten miles on a wave, Texas will get yet another record. And since tanker surfing started in Houston, as far as we can tell, Texas deserves that much more credit. Well, let's give the credit to Texas surfers so crazy they'll brave polluted waters and oil tankers for their ride.

> *I find golf stultifyingly dull. The only two good balls I ever hit was when I stepped on a garden rake.*
> *– Kinky Friedman, Honorary Texan, singer, occasional politician*

### Rodeo Bits

Rodeo became the official Texas State Sport in 1997, and joined the states of Wyoming and South Dakota as honoring the sport that way. But that recognition is several hundred

93

years late.

All rodeo events are based on activities of cattle herding. Rodeos started in Spain, spread to Mexico, and from there to Mexican territories like Texas. How did Wyoming and South Dakota glom onto rodeos? Big cattle herds led to Mexicans and Texans, and hence to rodeos.

How deeply rooted is rodeo in Mexican and Spanish roots? Let's look at the terms used…

**Vaquero** – combination of the Spanish words for cow and man.

**Chaps** – from chaparreras, the leather leggings worn to protect the wearer from cactus and brush (and that Village People singer from adoring fans).

**Lasso** – from lazo

**Ranch** – from rancho

**Rodeo** – from rodear, the Spanish term that means to encircle a herd.

**Vamoose** – from vamos, which means "let's go" as in "let's go to the rodeo."

The Canadian province Alberta also has a big rodeo following. That makes more sense when you look at a map and see it's near Wyoming. And why does the Professional Rodeo Cowboys Association hold their National Finals Rodeo in Las Vegas? Because showgirls love their cowboys.

Why do the San Antonio Spurs basketball team NBA champions in 1999, 2003, 2005, and 2007, get run out of town each year for an extended road trip? The rodeo needs their building, and the rodeo wins.

When you talk to your Hispanic friends about rodeo, be prepared to get ribbed a bit. After all, vaquero translates to "cow man" while in English the term is "cow boy."

## Bob Belts #1,000,000

The one-millionth run in Major League Baseball was scored in the Houston Astrodome in 1975. Bob Watson ran like the dickens on May 4, 1975, because there were other games going on around the league, and he wanted to get the credit for run #1,000,000. Congrats, Bob.

Twenty years later, Bob returned to Houston and the Astros as the first African-American general manager in MLB. He stayed for a year, and then moved to the New York Yankees in 1995. The Yankees won their first World Series since 1978 the next year, Bob's second. Congrats, Bob.

> *Lord, don't remove any stumbling blocks. Just give me strength.*
> *– Earl Campbell, UT and Houston Oilers star running back*

## The Ryan Express

Lynn Nolan Ryan Jr., born January 31, 1947, in Refugio, Texas, grew up in Alvin about 35 miles south of Houston. Folks noticed his right arm early, including Major League Baseball scouts, and he was drafted by the New York Mets right out of Alvin High School in 1965. He threw his last pitch on September 22, 1993.

In between, he was an All-Star eight times, stuck out more batters (5,714) than anyone ever had, and pitched seven no-hitters. Less well known are his 12 one-hitters and 18 two-hitters.

The Houston Astros signed Ryan for the 1980 season and he stayed there through 1988. He threw his fifth no-hitter there, as well as his 3,000th and 4,000th strikeouts. But Houston felt he was too old and balked at contract time after the 1988 season, and Ryan zoomed up the road to the Texas Rangers in Arlington.

As a Ranger, Ryan got his 5,000th strikeout. Ricky Henderson, the victim, took it well. "If he ain't struck you out, then you ain't nobody," said Henderson.

One of Ryan's most high profile events in the mainstream

press was a fight on August 4, 1993. He had announced that was his last year (27 years in baseball is quite a ride) and planned to retire. But on that August night, he hit 26-year-old Robin Ventura of the Chicago White Sox with a pitch. Ventura seemed to think about it, and then charged the mound.

In video that will live forever, Ryan calmly waited for Ventura to make it to the mound. Then, far quicker than Ventura could have expected from a man 20 years his senior, Ryan grabbed Ventura in a headlock with the left arm and started wailing away on Ventura's face with his right fist. Yep, Ventura spotted Ryan 20 years, and senior whupped junior like a rented mule. Since Ryan hadn't run away from the mound, the umpire let him stay in the game, but ejected Ventura. No doubt Robin needed to go get a bag of ice for his knuckle-bruised face, and a truckload of ice for his manhandled reputation. Luckily, Ryan didn't hurt has hand while repeatedly punching Ventura, and finished (and won) the game.

On September 22 that year, just two starts away from his planned retirement, Ryan tore a ligament in his pitching arm. Wanting to continue despite the injury, Ryan kept pitching. The next pitch, with a torn ligament, was still 98 miles per hour. But he couldn't go on, and that was the end.

Nolan Ryan was the last ballplayer from the 1960s to retire from the Major Leagues. By the end, he played with several sons of teammates from early in his career.

Now the president of the Texas Rangers, Ryan still stands tall in baseball. Unfortunately, he never got a World Series ring, although the Rangers did get to the World Serious in 2010, only to lose to the San Francisco Giants. But Ryan was deservedly inducted into the Baseball Hall of Fame on the first ballot in 1999, six votes short of a unanimous election.

## *The Cotton Bowl*

When Texans think of football games on New Year's Day, they think of the Cotton Bowl in Dallas' Fair Park. The first attempt to build a stadium in Fair Park failed in the 1890's, but succeeded in 1921, and was replaced by a bigger one in 1930, boosting seating from 15,000 to 46,000.

The first official Cotton Bowl Classic took place on January 1, 1937, between the Horned Frogs of Texas Christian University and Marquette University. The locals (well, Fort Worth is closer to Dallas than Milwaukee, Wisconsin) prevailed, 16-6. Organizer and oilman J. Curtis Sanford gets credit for the bowl name, but he lost over $6,000 on the game (his accountants claim that was a business loss, not a crazy bet on Marquette over the Horned Frogs).

Losing money on football, with or without illegal wagering, was common at that time. The name "Cotton Bowl Classic" became replaced by "Sanford's Folly" in the minds of many, and losing money on each game every year didn't help Mr. Sanford's reputation as a clever businessman. It wasn't until he hooked up with the Southwest Conference that Sanford started actually making money, selling over 45,000 tickets to the Texas A&M and Fordham University game in 1941. From then on, Sanford was, as they say, in high cotton.

The Dallas Cowboys started playing their professional games (that's a charitable description for their early years) in the Cotton Bowl 1960, as did the Dallas Texans. Losing the battle for the few professional football fans around, the Texans gave up and moved to Kansas City in 1962 and became the Chiefs. The original Dallas Texans started playing professionally (again, a kindly description) in the Cotton Bowl in 1952, but they lost money and moved to Baltimore. With a record like that, fans everywhere should be happy the Cowboys avoided that curse and survived.

Of course, the Cowboys thrived, and moved to Texas Stadium in Irving, Texas, in 1971, and then to the most expensive stadium in the world, Cowboys Stadium, in Arlington, in 2009. In fact, the 74th game of the AT&T Cotton Bowl Classic, where the Ole Miss Rebels beat the Oklahoma

State Cowboys 31-7, occurred not at the Cotton Bowl in Fair Park but at the new Cowboys Stadium. The Honchos and Honchettes of the Texas Hysterical Society declare playing the "Cotton Bowl" somewhere besides the actual Cotton Bowl to be money grubbing and bad behavior of the worst sort. You change the stadium, you change the Bowl Game name. Harrumph.

## Cowboys Stadium

If it's football, and it's Texas, it should be the biggest and best. And the new Cowboys Stadium has won praise from all quarters for the stadium itself and the world's largest video display screens.

Everyone remembers Texas Stadium, in Irving (a suburb abutting Dallas), that opened in 1971. The open roof protected the fans to some degree, and allowed nice TV shots from the blimp. It also spawned bad jokes (the hole was there so God could watch his favorite football team).

Forty years is a lifetime for a high tech football palace, and Jerry Jones (Honorary Texan) started planning a new football palace back in 1997 (these things take a long, long time to design and build). Although one would think the Dallas Cowboys would want to play inside the city of Dallas, that just shows one's inexperience with the way high football finance is done.

Yes, the Cowboys talked to the City of Dallas leaders about putting their huge new stadium in Fair Park, replacing and updating the Cotton Bowl. Alas, Dallas city leaders, forever small minded and short of vision, balked at having to put up any money for the project. To be fair, the price of the public part of the stadium at that time was $425 Million (with an M), which hit at a bad time in 2003 as things were still a bit dicey from the 2001-2 recession.

Arlington, home of the Six Flags theme part and the Texas Rangers, had the vision to take the lead in the race to host the stadium. In 2004, the deal was done, hands were shaken, and eminent domain orders started flying to remove houses in the way. Football palaces, like churches, are exempt from zoning laws and can be put anywhere.

Word on the business street is that no company would pay as much for the rights to name the stadium as Jerry Jones wanted. Cleverly, Jones named it Cowboys Stadium, so if a corporate sponsor does want to make it the, say, Dairy Queen Dome, most people will still call it Cowboys Stadium.

> *It takes a lot of unspectacular preparation to get spectacular results.*
> *– Roger Staubach, Honorary Texan*

The football field is limited to 100 yards, but nothing else limited the size and scale of Cowboys Stadium. Most of the news focused on the video screens, and it's hard not to. The main video screen assembly weighs 600 tons (that's 1.2 million pounds). The high definition screen from Mitsubishi Diamond Vision is 60 yards long (over half the football field), 72 feet tall, and has about 30 million LEDs. On each end, the "small" screens are 29 by 51 feet. Besides the four huge screens, there are about 2,900 other video screens around the place.

Money? How about $1.3 Billion, with a B, dollars. Give Jerry credit, because the public put up only about $325 million, much less than many areas have to pay as a percentage of the total costs. See, Dallas? For $325 million you could have the bragging rights to the biggest football stadium in the world.

In April 2006, dirt started flying. Lots of dirt. The bowl of the stadium is 54 feet deep on average, and over 1.4 million cubic yards of dirt was cleared out to create 13 acres of space.

George Strait and Reba McEntire, two county music superstars, performed first in Cowboys Stadium on May 27, 2009. Hard to believe it took only three years from first shovel to welcoming the public, but this is Texas. Big things happen fast around here.

It appears Cowboys Stadium can do just about everything. Football, of course, including professional, college, and high school playoffs. Music concerts. The first point scored was a soccer goal by Costa Rica in the Gold Cup Quarterfinal game with Guadeloupe. The 2010 NBA All Star game was held there (boy, did they have trouble dribbling that ball on the turf). Since Cowboys Stadium can hold way more than 100,000 fans, the crowd of 108,713 was, of course, a new Guinness World Record for basketball attendance. Who won the game? Who cares, it's an All Star Game (East 141-139 over the West).

If you get a chance to see Cowboys Stadium, take it. But if you go to a game, bring a bucket of money. Jerry has to pay for that $1.3 Billion football palace somehow. Unfortunately for Jerry and the cities of Dallas, Fort Worth, and Arlington, the Super Bowl on February 6, 2011, brought more bad weather than tourists. However, since the teams in the Super Bowl were the Green Bay Packers and the Pittsburgh Steelers, the weather in Texas was warmer than the weather back home. But not by much. And in a nice linking of southern traditions, the Super Bowl halftime entertainment was by the Black Eyed Peas (the music group, not the black-eyed peas of side dish fame).

### Non-official nicknames for Cowboys Stadium

**JerryWorld** (the most common snide media reference today)
**JonesTown** (here, opponents, have some Kool-Aid)
**JerryDome** (would work better if Jerry was bald)
**JonesMahal** (nice international touch)
**Death Star** (that would certainly chill opponents)
**The Palace in Dallas** (oops, not quite in Dallas)
**Boss Hog Bowl** (Jerry Jones played football for the University of Arkansas and is therefore a Razorback Hog)
**Six Flags over Jerry** (wonder where they got that idea?)
**FedoraBowl** (in honor of longtime Cowboy coach Tom Landry)

## *Organic Fundraising*

Fundraising for schools takes many forms. There's bake sales, raffle tickets, silent auctions, and maybe even planting a flock of pink plastic flamingos in yards and charging money to remove them in a reverse kidnap charity scheme. But only in Texas can you charge 900 people to sit in a football stadium watching a bull. And not just watching, but hoping the bull plops a big wet one down in a particular place.

That was the scene in 2005 at Lake Travis High School, when their third annual event raised over $75,000 for the school's athletic fund. People bought t-shirts, ate barbecue, played games, listened to a local rock band, and finally, as the grand finale, watched Mr. International, a 2,000-pound Brahma bull, enter the stadium. Then they held their breath, but started breathing again, because Mr. International loved the spotlight so much he wandered around the field for 45 minutes before he decided to do what he was being paid to do: poop.

The man who chose the two-foot by two-foot square where Mr. International finally did the deed won $2,500 in gift certificates. No mention was made of how much they had to pay to clean up the field after Mr. International exited stage left.

Old timers will recognize this as the much bigger brother of a popular county fair game called Chicken S#*t Bingo. Explain that one to some Yankees when you have a chance, and that cheering people hang around the game watching caged chickens "mark" the bingo cards.

## *The Pedernales Golf Club*

Texas golf fanatics know about the Pedernales Golf Club, but they know it by the more Texan name of Willie Nelson's Cut-n-Putt. Located in Spicewood, Texas, not too far west of Austin, Willie's Cut-n-Putt course also has a recording studio, condos, and more than a little golfing fun.

All golf clubs have rules, but none like these. Here are the official rules, straight from Willie and the website (pedernalesgolfclub.com):

1. When another player is shooting, no player should talk, whistle, hum, clink coins, or pass gas.
2. Don't play until the group in front is out of the way.
3. Excessive displays of affection are discouraged. Violators must replace divots and will be penalized five strokes.
4. Replace divots, smooth footprints in bunkers, brush backtrail with branches, park car under brush, and have the office tell your spouse you're in a conference.
5. Let faster groups play through.
6. On the putting green, don't step on another's line.
7. "Freebies" are not recommended for players with short putts.
8. No more than twelve in your foursome.
9. Gambling is forbidden, of course, unless you're stuck or you need a legal deduction for charitable or educational expenses.
10. All carts are not allowed within 20 ft. of traps or aprons surrounding greens.
11. No bikinis, mini-skirts, skimpy see-through, or sexually exploitative attire allowed. Except on women.
12. Please leave course in the condition in which you would like for it to be found.

Hard to pick your favorite rule, isn't it? Many are partial to Number 11, but our love of wordplay makes Number 8 special.

Willie fell in love with the course after a celebrity tournament in the mid 1970s. He and a partner bought it in 1979, Willie let him have it, then bought it back. During his well-publicized IRS troubles, Willie lost the course to the Feds. Legendary UT football coach Darrell Royal bought the course at auction, but the IRS claimed it wasn't enough and took it back and sold it to someone else. Willie didn't like that someone else, so he convinced a Branson, Missouri, theater owner to buy it, and give it back to Willie in exchange for about six months of shows. Few people have bought the same golf club in as many ways as Willie has bought the Pedernales Golf Club.

> *Par at my golf course is whatever I say it is. Today I made a fourteen on the first hole and it turned out to be a birdie.*
> *— Willie Nelson, Honorary Texan*
> *(friends say Willie would pick up his ball before shooting a fourteen, but let's not ruin a good quote)*

Willie's favorite house sits on the golf course. His recording studio is located next to the clubhouse. Not surprisingly, the décor in the clubhouse is memorabilia from Willie's career.

Another "fun" rule is the Pedernales Stroll, created to smooth out the rough course terrain. "In case your ball ends up in an unplayable or merely unpleasant lie, the local rules permit you to pick it up and stroll to a more agreeable location for a free drop." No, there are never arguments about the lie, the length of stroll, or the ball drop. Never. At least not with pistols.

### Shelby Metcalf

Shelby Metcalf, the basketball coach at Texas A&M from 1963 to 1990, checked his athlete's report cards regularly. When he saw one that had four F's and a D, he told the student-athlete, "Son, it looks like you're spending too much time on one subject."

During a game, he asked the referee if he could get a technical foul for what he was thinking. The referee said no, so Metcalf answered, "Well, I'm thinking you're a jackass."

Though Coach Metcalf was born in Oklahoma, in respect

for his long service to Texas A&M, he's officially granted the status of Honorary Texan.

Shelby Metcalf couldn't always keep his wit from landing himself in the, ah, poop. He one said about John David Crow, the legendary Texas A&M football star and later Athletic Director, "I made a comment that I didn't think John David was all that bright. And I thought I was being generous." Little slips like that led to John David smartly swinging the job ax on Shelby.

> *Three blind mice are not any better than two blind mice.*
> *— Shelby Metcalf, Honorary Texan*

His answer when a sportswriter asked Metcalf what he thought of the league adding a third official to help control basketball games.

# Women
# and
# Men

## Bless Your Heart

A polite, gentle, God-fearing, and "well seasoned" Texas woman was driving across a high bridge over the Colorado River not far from Austin one day. In the center of the bridge, she saw a young man climbing on the railing.

She pulled up near him, stopped, and rolled down her window. "Young man, are you all right?" she called.

"I'm going to jump, and you can't stop me," he said, inching his way to the edge.

"Please don't," she said, "Remember your dear mother, and your dear father."

"They're both dead."

"Please remember your wife and children."

"I don't have any kids, and my wife just left me. Another reason you can't stop me."

Sitting up straighter and speaking with more authority, the woman yelled, "Remember the Alamo!"

The man stopped, and the woman hoped she had dissuaded him from his plans. But he looked at her curiously and asked, "What's the Alamo?"

Shaking her head, the gentle Texas lady said, "Well, bless your heart. Go ahead and jump, you dumbass Yankee!"

---

*Definition: When a Texas woman, or any woman raised in the South, says, "Bless your heart," she's being polite, but not in the way you think. She is not wishing you well, she is using a code phrase that really means "you are amazingly stupid."*

---

Marvin was in his usual place in the morning sitting at the table, reading the paper after breakfast. He came across an article about a beautiful actress that was about to marry a football player who was known primarily for his lack of IQ, common sense, and civility.

He turned to his wife with a look of question on his face. "I'll never understand why the biggest jerks get the most attractive wives."

His wife replied, "Thank you, dear!"

## *The Boot from Enid*

Enid Justin was overlooked in 1894, when she was one of seven children of Herman J. Justin of Nocona, Texas. Her father had built up his handmade boot business started in 1879 with the help of Enid's mother and several brothers. In fact, the two oldest boys, John and Earl, became full partners in 1908 and the company name was changed to H. J. Justin and Sons, not H. J. Justin and Children. H. J. died in 1918, leaving Enid's two older brothers in charge of everything.

By 1925, the boot company had grown so much the Industrial Board of the Fort Worth Chamber of Commerce lured them out of Nocona to the big city of Fort Worth. Enid, a stubborn young woman, thought moving away from Nocona and the handcrafted boots was a mistake. The boys wanted more automation, but Enid wanted to keep the personal touch and high quality. After all, at age 10 she started working in the family business, and dropped out of school to stitch boots in the factory at age 12, so she knew of what she spoke.

Enid and seven employees started the Nocona Boot Company with $5,000 in borrowed money in 1926. Before long, she was Justin Boot's biggest competitor (see what happens when you aggravate a Texas woman?). Some men didn't like boots made by a woman, but others found Enid quite convincing. As the oil boom ramped in up West Texas, Enid became a saleswoman extraordinaire and built up a strong business. The Great Depression slowed them down, but she started selling boots outside Texas in 1934. When the economy recovered, so did Nocona Boots, until World War II crimped their supplies of leather and other materials.

After the war, things took off so well Enid built a bigger

107

factory. All things cowboy were becoming popular in films and TV, and that certainly helped. In 1977 Enid opened a second factory in Vernon Texas. In 1981 she let her brother's old boot company, Justin Industries, buy her out (she was 87, after all).

Don't you know Enid loved getting that big check for the company her brothers told her she was stupid for opening? Let that be a lesson to all people with a younger sister: underestimate them at your peril. They watched you grow up and could thereby avoid the mistakes they saw you making. And being a woman selling boots to oil field and construction workers didn't hurt Enid, either.

The Old Cowgirl lay in the emergency room as the doctors poked and prodded and tested. After a few minutes, one doctor came out to the waiting room.

"I don't like the looks of your wife at all."

"Me neither, Doc," said the Old Cowboy. "But she's a great cook and really good with the kids."

> *A major advantage of age is learning to accept people without passing judgment.*
> *— Liz Carpenter*
> *Journalist and later Press Secretary*
> *for Lady Bird Johnson*
>
> *Being a dating woman is like being a bank teller...: Next!*
> *— Donna K. Martin, writer*
>
> *Live your life in such a way that you have great stories to tell.*
> *— Jo Virgil, Community Outreach and Information*
> *Coordinator for the Texas Governor's*
> Committee on People with Disabilities.

> *When you make a mistake, especially with a woman, fix it immediately. Crow is easier to eat when warm.*
>
> *– The Old Cowboy*

## A New Interpretation of the Facts

Sometimes you learn things about yourself in strange ways.

One day an old cowboy stopped at a McDonald's to get some coffee. As he sat there, a pretty young woman sat down by him. He smiled, and she smiled back.

Curious, she turned to him and asked, "Are you a real cowboy?"

"Well, ma'am," he answered. "I've spent all my days riding horses, training horses, fixing fences, chasing cows, branding cows, and riding in rodeos. So, I guess that makes me a real cowboy."

The woman nodded. "Well, I'm a lesbian. I've spent all my days thinking about naked women. When I get up, I think about naked women. When I shower I think about naked women. When I watch TV, I imagine all the beautiful women on the shows naked."

Nodding, the cowboy sipped his coffee, and the woman sipped soda. After a couple of silent moments, a young man sat on the other side of the cowboy.

"Excuse me, but are you a real cowboy? Like from a ranch and stuff?"

"I always thought I was, but it turns out I'm a lesbian."

Lawrence, a New Yorker fascinated with all things Texans, booked himself a dude ranch vacation. The first day, he arrived early at the corral to get a roping lesson.

"This here's a lariat," said the cowboy instructor.

Lawrence took notes carefully. "What is a lariat for?"

"We use it to catch cows."

Lawrence nodded and got his pen ready. "And what do you use for bait?"

> *Men say, "I'll talk at you later" because they plan to impart information in the future. Women say, "Let's talk soon" because they want to share their feelings and crap.*
> *— The Old Cowboy*

A cowboy asked an old Indian what his wife's name was. "She named Four Horse."

"Interesting. Is that because of some kind of dowry, or a family name, or what?"

"Old Indian name. Really means nag, nag, nag, nag."

One day at an extended family reunion, grandparents sat reminiscing. One grandfather remarked, "I wonder what happened to the old fashioned girls who fainted when a man kissed them?"

Several of the grandmothers gave him a look. One finally said, "I wonder what happened to the old fashioned men who made them faint?"

> *Deja Moo: the feeling you've heard this bull before.*

A young woman on a business trip to Dallas, full of romantic notions about cowboys, headed to a country music bar after her meetings. She planned to put test the rumor she'd heard that the bigger the cowboy's boots in relation to his body size, the bigger his "equipment." And as always happens when a pretty girl is determined, even a Yankee girl, she picked the cowboy she wanted and took him back to her hotel.

The next morning, she stopped the cowboy as he was leaving and gave him $100 bill. Flustered, he said, "Shuck's ma'am, you don't owe me nothing. The pleasure was all mine."

"Exactly," she said. "Go buy yourself a pair of boots that fit properly."

> *Remember, nowadays you can hit the undo button and just about everything will be all right. If not, reboot; step into your boots and kick the hell out of the panic button!*
> *— Becky Chavarria-Chairez, author*

In order to finally enjoy life the way it should be enjoyed, Ray and Rhonda moved to Texas after they retired. Trying to fit in, Ray went out the first week and bought a brand new pair of cowboy boots.

Eager to show them off, Ray walked into the house and asked Rhonda, "Notice anything different about me?"

Rhonda looked, shook her head, and said, "Nope."

Determined to draw attention to his boots, Ray stomped into the bedroom and removed all his clothes, then put the boots back on. Proudly he strode back over to Rhonda and asked once again, "Notice anything different about me?"

Rhonda looked up and laughed. "Oh, Ray, it was hanging down yesterday, it's handing down today, and it will hang down tomorrow."

Ray couldn't take it anymore. "It's hanging down because it's looking at my new cowboy boots!"

Rhonda smiled. "Then quit wasting time, Ray, and go buy a damn cowboy hat!"

## Weapon of choice: Mercedes.

In July, 2002, Dr. Clara Harris, a dentist, tracked her cheating husband, Dr. David Harris, to the Hilton NASA Clear Lake hotel in Nassau Bay, Texas. After confronting her husband in the lobby, they took their argument outside, in the best Texas tradition.

In an unusual twist on the "let's go outside and settle this" argument escalation, Dr. Clara jumped in her Mercedes and accidentally ran down Dr. David. Accidentally. Several times. Then once more for good measure.

Dr. Clara admitted the deed during questioning. Add in the fact her stepdaughter, the daughter of Dr. David, was in the car with her, and that pretty much sealed the deal for the police.

Texas courts being the way they are sometimes, Dr. Clara was released on a $30,000 bond. After all, this was just an interoffice squabble, since Dr. David's mistress was a receptionist at one of their dental clinics.

But Dr. Clara wasn't Texan: she was born in Columbia, and a one-time beauty contest winner. She also, not surprisingly, still claims it was all an accident. Where did the good doctors live, before the murder and Dr. Clara's 20 year prison sentence? An expensive Houston suburb named Friendswood, Texas.

> *You're only young once, but you can stay immature forever.*
> *— The Old Cowboy*
>
> *Especially if you're male.*
> *— The Old Cowgirl*

A Texas woman knows that no matter how accomplished he is, every man who marries a Texas woman marries above himself. She also knows that will be true for her sons. But since Texas women are the absolute best women in the world, her sons will be happy.

"When we get married, I want to share all your worries, soothe your troubles, and lighten your burden," said the young cowgirl.

"That's sweet, darlin', but I don't have any worries, troubles, or burdens," said the young cowboy.

"That's because we ain't married yet."

A man decided to save his wife some trouble and wash his own sweatshirt after mowing the yard. Ten seconds after entering the laundry room, he yelled out to his wife, "What setting do I use on the washer?"

"It depends," she answered. "What does it say on your sweatshirt?"

"Texas A&M."

A young cowboy whistled at a pretty young cowgirl as she walked by, her tight boot-cut blue jeans emphasizing the swing of her hips enhanced by the high heels on her boots.

"Wow, I sure would like to get into them pants," he said.

"Great," she answered without stopping or turning to look at him. "Then I'll have two assholes in there."

*Deja Moo: the feeling you've heard this bull before.*

A pretty young woman came home from a date with her long-time boyfriend and immediately started crying on her mother's shoulder.

"Did Darrell do something mean to you, baby?" her mother asked.

"No," the young woman sobbed. "In fact, he asked me to marry him."

"That's wonderful. So why are you crying?"

"Because you raised me in the church," said the young woman, drying her eyes. "Darrell wasn't, and he says he's an atheist. He doesn't even believe there's a hell."

"That's OK," said her mother. "Marry him. The two of us will show him how wrong he is."

AshleyMadison.com, a dating service for married people (who are not married to each other) that proclaims "life is short, have an affair" on their Web site tried to advertise on the 2009 Super Bowl. Forty-nine states banned the commercial. Texas, however, didn't. This either means that the Texas Powers That Be assumed responsible Texas adults could think for themselves about such a personal issue, or that they thought Ashley Madison was the company making those cute dolls.

We at the Texas Hysterical Society suspect the latter.

> *Marriage is, perhaps, the only game of chance ever invented at which it is possible for both players to lose.*
> *– William Cowper Brann, Honorary Texan*

As the graveside funeral service ended, the mourners heard a tremendous clap of thunder. The Old Cowboy turned to the minister and said, "She's there."

> *Married men live a lot longer than single men, but married men are also much more willing to die.*
> *– The Old Cowboy*

No Texas woman has ever shot her husband while he was doing housework. Men, if you screw up big time, grab a mop and keep cleaning until she starts smiling.

# Geography
# and
# Weather

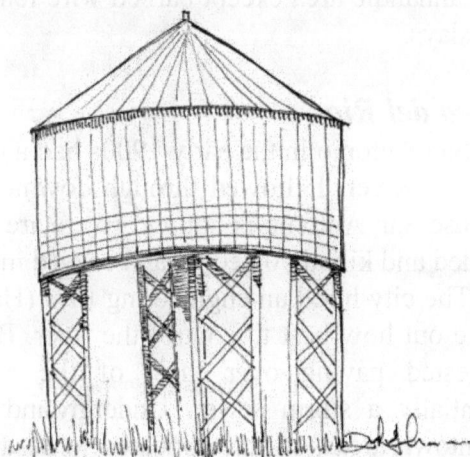

## Highs and Lows

Two towns hit a high of 120 degrees in Texas, although many towns feel like they hover around that temperature most summer days. First, Seymour, in North West Texas, hit that painful milestone on August 12, 1936. In case you think the old thermometer may have been reading hot, Monahans, also in West Texas, hit 120 degrees on June 28, 1994. By that time the TV stations in nearby Odessa had weathermen wearing bow ties and weather girls wearing short dresses, so that's legit.

The coldest winter on record was in 1898-1899. During that chilly time, Tulia, also in West Texas, dropped all the way down to -23 degrees (23 degrees below zero, or 56 degrees below freezing).

All the fun weather seems to happen in west Texas or the Panhandle. One snowstorm in 1956 dropped 33 inches on Hale Center over four days. Romero, not that far away, had 65 inches of snow dumped on them during the 1923-1924 winter. Those Canadian storms whistle down from the north, bouncing off the Rockies on their way down, and there's nothing stopping the frigid air from whamming into West Texas and the Panhandle area except barbed wire fences. Makes for some cold days.

## Paseo del Rio

San Antonio in the early 1900s had a problem with the San Antonio River. It flowed through downtown, which was nice because San Antonio is hot and rivers are cool. But in 1921, it flooded and killed 50 people and caused millions in damages.

The city hired an engineering firm (Hawley and Freese) to figure out how best to control the river. Being engineers, they suggested paving over most of the river and making it essentially a storm sewer. Underground sewers don't flood downtown areas, so this appeared to be a great solution to an engineering problem.

Fortunately, people who weren't engineers thought that a horrible way to hide a great natural resource. Groups organized to save the river after city officials gave a thumbs up to keeping the river down and out of sight. River advocates (early environmentalists?) made enough noise that the city reconsidered.

> *Texas could wear Rhode Island as a watch fob.*
> *– Pat Neff, Texas governor 1921-1925*

In 1929 architect Robert H. H. Hugman pitched the idea of making the river area an urban park with all types of dollar magnets like bars, restaurants, shops, hotels, and apartments. Hugman was the only one with the vision to see Venice in Texas, including boats for travel up and down the river.

Hugman kept up the pitch and by the 1930s some other civic groups could see the vision of Venice in Texas. Businesses on the river promised to pony up the extra pennies per foot of river footage, but the city officials nixed the idea. There's nothing like a budget shortfall to cause city officials to close their eyes to visions of civic improvement.

Luckily for San Antonio, the nation was in the Great Depression (don't often see "lucky" and "Great Depression" in the same sentence, do you?). The Feds, in the form of the Works Projects Administration, provided $355,000 dollars in a grant to extend a new tax of 1.5 cents per $100 and $75,000 in bonds. Shovels appeared and dirt flew, or rather water and mud splashed. Over 11,700 trees and shrubs were planted

All was well by 1941, except for the part about tourist traffic being drawn to the Riverwalk (Paseo del Rio). Criminals and vagrants loved the Riverwalk, driving tourists and locals away. Casa Rio, a wonderful Tex-Mex restaurant, opened on the Riverwalk in 1946 and still sells great food today, but they also had an upstairs dining room and street entrance, and were the first business to open on the Riverwalk proper.

> *How windy is it in west Texas? One farmer reported his chicken laid the same egg four times.*

Civic salvation came in the form of Hemisfair '68. Planning began early, and the San Antonio Riverwalk Commission organized in 1962 to prepare for tourists flocking to the area with wallets full of cash. Lighting was improved, more shops and restaurants opened, and everything was cleaned up. The Riverwalk became a success.

Ever since then, the Riverwalk has been a tourist magnet and home to an increasing number of businesses. Anything that gets you out of the sun in a San Antonio summer deserves to do well, and the Riverwalk offers shade, history, food, drink, music, plays, clothing stores, and even narrated boat rides. They've even added extra loops of Riverwalk over the past few years, a sure sign of success.

Today the Rivercenter shopping mall and fancy hotel draws tourists, along with the seemingly unending number of bars, restaurants, and stores along the miles of river walkways. The tour boats carry thousands people per day, and, each year the San Antonio Spurs won the NBA Championship, they had a "parade" on the boats down the Riverwalk. Nearly a billion dollars of tourist money stays in San Antonio each year thanks to what could have been a covered sewer.

## Here's Dust in Your Eye

The Dust Bowl of the mid to late 1930s started in West Texas and covered parts of New Mexico, Oklahoma's Panhandle, western Kansas, and even some of the eastern Colorado. Total area affected was about 100 million acres. Texas and Oklahoma got the worst of it.

NASA scientists doing a 100 year climate study found the likely cause: cooler than normal tropical Pacific Ocean surface temperatures working in tandem with warmer than normal tropical Atlantic Ocean temperatures. This condition pushed the large-scale weather patterns off-kilter, lowering the amount of moisture in the area that usually came up from the Gulf of Mexico. The painful result was less rain in the Dust Bowl areas that created a veritable desert. Not that ignoring climate change today will cause any problems tomorrow. History has nothing to teach us, right?

The stronger than normal winds found plenty of dust to blow around, because farming methods changed the ground environment for the worse just before the weather patterns shifted to keep humidity out of the area. Grasslands, which held the dirt in place, were overstocked with cattle herds, which ate the grass.

Worse, "the great plow-up," powered by the newfangled gasoline tractors, turned under millions of acres of grassland to prepare for traditional "rows of crops" farming. Wheat production jumped until there was a peak followed by a glut that devastated the market, in 1931. Broke wheat farmers didn't plant any more wheat, leaving the ground unprotected. Cotton farmers left their fields bare during the winter, and many burned the stubble as a form of weed control. Less organic material in the fields means more erosion and fuel for the dust storms.

Unusually wet weather earlier had convinced the experts that the dusty, arid area really could support intensive agriculture. Too bad weather patterns change.

Between the overgrazing, plowing under, failed wheat farms, and speculation, more than a third of the eventual Dust Bowl area was bare, unprotected ground. When the "black blizzards" started up thanks to the shifting wind patterns, topsoil from millions of acres provided the raw material. The grasses that had held the moisture and dirt in place for thousands of years were gone, and the dirt just blew away. With each dust storm, the Dust Bowl became more arid and received less rain.

> *Never ride a horse named Whiplash, Backbreaker, or Widowmaker.*
>
> *– The Old Cowboy*

Losing millions of acres of farmland during the Depression just seems like Mother Nature piled on and deserves a penalty for unnecessary roughness. But smarter farming methods and better weather tracking makes some experts swear the Dust Bowl should be relegated to history (dry, dry, history). Other experts point out that dust storms in the mid-1950s and 1970s prove we're not as smart as we think we are. Or that Mother Nature can really be unpleasant at times.

Global warming worriers point out that less than a two degree rise in global temperatures will restart the Dust Bowl. Australia, after a major drought for seven years, had a truly Texas-sized dust storm in 2009, then horrible floods in 2010 (that would turn an Australian Dust Bowl into a Mud Bowl, mate). China is currently turning one million acres of good land into desert each year. They've had some Texas-sized sandstorms already, and will see some more if the trend continues.

We at the Texas Hysterical Society are just glad the people forced westward to California by the Dust Bowl were labeled Okies.

## The Dangerous Border

"Juarez is reported to be the most dangerous city in America." So said Governor Rick Perry, in a speech criticizing the Obama administration's failure to protect the border. Governor Good Hair is correct: the United States does nothing to stop Mexicans from going to Juarez.

## *Hippo Capitol of the World – Hutto, Texas*

So declared the Texas State Legislature a few years ago in honor of the hippo-crazed town of Hutto, Texas. Why? There are concrete hippos all over town, as many as 87 in public places at last count.

In 1915, the circus came through town, and one the hippos made a break for freedom. Hey, even hippos love Texas, especially Cottonwood Creek, where the illegal alien hippo hid for a couple of days. As luck would have it, the town of Hutto was having a slow news day, and the hippo became a celebrity. Residents at the time said Hutto always had slow news days, so just about any escaped animal would have made news, except maybe a mule. The fact that their new citizen was an alliterative Hutto Hippo was just whipped cream and a cherry on top of a great surprise.

Hutto is about 22 miles northeast of Austin and has been booming from 1,250 people in the 2000 census to about 17,120 people in 2008. Suburban sprawl will do that to you. Having a town full of hippos that makes Hutto stand out in the competition for new citizens in bedroom communities doesn't hurt the growth, either.

Wander around and see the hippos, many dressed, or painted, or covered in graffiti. Go see the local high school, home of the Hustlin' Hippos. And get in arguments with the locals, half of whom love the hippos, and half of whom hate them.

Relax, haters. The escaped circus animal could have been a hyena, and those aren't a bit whimsical nor nearly as cute as concrete hippos.

### *You know it's summer in Texas when ...*

- Birds use potholders to pull worms out of the ground.
- Trees whistle for dogs.
- Your car-parking place is determined by shade, not

121

proximity to your destination.
- You learn cars can be steered with two fingers.
- Seat belt buckles become branding irons.
- You get sunburned through your car windows.
- Opening the car door gives you a second degree burn.
- Your biggest worry while riding a bicycle is that you may fall and get cooked before you can get up off the pavement.
- You learn asphalt has a liquid state.
- Potatoes cook underground, and you can make dinner by digging one up, adding butter, sour cream, and a few bacon sprinkles, then putting it directly on the plate.
- Farmers feed their chickens ice so they don't lay hard boiled eggs.
- The catfish have fleas.
- Cows give evaporated milk.
- You start sweating when you step outside – at 7:30 A.M.
- You make sun tea instantly.
- Hot water comes out of both taps.
- No matter how long you run the garden hose outside, it never gets cool enough to drink the water.

The highest point in Texas is Guadalupe Peak with an elevation of 8,749 feet. The lowest point is officially sea level, at the actual SEA where Texas ends at the Gulf of Mexico. The average elevation in Texas is about 1,700 feet.

If you worry about volcanoes or earthquakes, move to Texas and stop worrying. There are no active volcanoes, and darn few earthquakes, none of which are big enough to make the news. Big Bend is the most active area all types of seismic activity, which makes sense because that's what causes mountains in the first place.

On the other hand, you'll be safe from volcanoes but in danger from the large number of tornadoes anywhere in the state, and hurricanes close to the coast. You pays yer money, you takes yer chances.

## Marfa Mystery Lights

The South Texas town of Marfa, or at least the spot nine miles east of Marfa on Highway 90, has been discussed many times in various paranormal books. Lights, sometimes called Mystery Lights or Ghost Lights, have been spotted for about as long as people have been in the area.

Reports say the lights are spherical, seem to be one to 10 feet in diameter, and are mostly reddish-orange (or orangey red), but range from white to a brilliant red. They appear in the evening a few times a year, and some are stationary while others move around quite a bit, floating as high as 400 feet over the desert. Bright red lights disappear quickly. The lights tend to increase and decrease in intensity.

All manner of bizarre explanations have been presented, including Indian campfires in the late 1880s to automobile headlights being reflected through the cooling desert air. The more "interesting" explanations wander far further into paranormal territory (ghosts of old cowboys to a memorial for crashed aliens who didn't make it to Roswell, New Mexico) than we're comfortable accepting.

> El Paso is closer to California, two states away, than to Dallas.

Scientific explorations in the 1940s, 1950s, and later could never find the source. The most serious study, in 2004, set the cause as reflected headlights. Those scientists didn't explain how Robert Ellison reported them in 1883, before headlights.

The best, and most logical explanation, is piezoelectricity. Quartz concentrations are higher in the Marfa area than most others, and quartz crystals generate a voltage in response to stress. Days are hot, and the quartz and surrounding rocks expand. Desert temperatures drop fast when the sun sets, and the quartz contracts. That stress could generate the lights at night. Yes, there is similar but weaker stress in the morning as the sun warms the rocks, but it's hard to see subtle floating gobs of light in the daytime.

Don't let a potentially accurate yet dull explanation stop you from attending the Marfa Lights Festival on Labor Day Weekend. Come one, come all, and pay homage to the alien memorial marker (like the crosses you sometimes see beside highways. This is our favorite explanation).

Surf over to www.marfacc.com for the Chamber of Commerce website, and to www.marfa.org for less official but livelier information.

In some West Texas towns, part of the "going to school" traditions include a weather lesson. One teacher stands on the school roof with a water hose. The second teacher herds all the first graders out to the yard, then the first teacher sprays water up in the air and back down in front of the children.

"That," explains the second teacher, "is what rain looks like."

The Flagship Hotel in Galveston was the only hotel in North America built over water. We say "was" because Hurricane Ike blew it away in 2008.

The hurricane in 1900 that scoured Galveston Island almost completely clean and killed 6,000 to 8,000 people is the worst natural disaster in U.S. history. However, our friends to the east in New Orleans now beg to differ.

The Texas Flag can fly at the same height as the U.S. flag, the only state flag allowed to do so, because Texas became the 28th state by treaty, not annexation. Yes, we're special. In many ways.

***These are the six flags that have waved over Texas:***
Spain: 1519-1685 & 1690-1821
France: 1685-1690
Mexico: 1821-1836
Republic of Texas: 1836-1846
United States: 1846-1861 & 1865-Present
Confederacy: 1861-1865

***To balance the six flags, there have been six capital cities in Texas:***
Washington-on-the-Brazos
Harrisburg
Galveston
Velasco
West Columbia
Austin

A visitor out in west Texas asked an old cowboy, "Does it ever rain out here?"

"Sure, now and then," answered the cowboy.

The visitor looked around, surprised because he could see nothing but dirt covering everything, including all the plants and slow moving pets. "Really?"

"Sure," said the cowboy. "Remember that time in the Bible when it rained for 40 days and 40 nights?"

"Of course, Noah's flood."

"That time we got an inch and a half."

Dallas is the least "slow down and enjoy life" city in Texas, probably because there has never been oil found in Dallas County, so the city became overrun with executive bankers rather than salt of the earth roughnecks. This requires a different mindset while driving. If you actually slow down and stop at a yellow light, you may well be rear-ended and certainly cussed at. You may also be shot.

That traffic ticket for running the light doesn't look so expensive now, does it? Just hope the judge understands.

Many Texans are all in favor of global warming, but not for the reason you think. They believe if the glaciers actually melt, a giant fraud will be revealed. With the snow gone, everyone will see that Texas is actually bigger than Alaska. Texas will once again become the largest state in land mass. Texas has always been the largest state in presence, personality and impact, but reclaiming the largest physical size title would make Texans real happy.

> *Nobody but fools and newcomers dare to predict the weather in Texas.*
> *— The Old Cowboy*
>
> *That covers all the types of people in Texas.*
> *— The Newcomers*

## *A Town By Any Other Name*

Texas has more exciting, descriptive, and bizarre town names than any other state and most countries. Here's a good look at some great Texas town and city names:

**Emotional names:**
Comfort, Texas
Energy, Texas
Friendship, Texas
Paradise, Texas
Pep, Texas
Rainbow, Texas
Smiley, Texas
Sweet Home, Texas

**Get the dark glasses:**
Sun City, Texas
Sundown, Texas
Sunray, Texas
Sunrise, Texas
Sunset, Texas
Sunny Side, Texas

**Feeling peckish?**
Bacon, Texas
Noodle, Texas
Oatmeal, Texas
Orange, Texas
Pearland, Texas
Rice, Texas
Salty, Texas
Sugarland, Texas
Sweetwater, Texas
Trout, Texas
Turkey, Texas

**The world comes to Texas:**
Athens, Texas
Canadian, Texas
China, Texas
Egypt, Texas
Ireland, Texas
Italy, Texas
London, Texas
New London, Texas
Paris, Texas
Palestine, Texas
Turkey, Texas
(the penultimate town on this list is pronounced "pal-uh-steen")

**The nation comes to Texas:**
Boston, Texas
Cleveland, Texas
Colorado City, Texas
Columbus, Texas
Denver City, Texas
Detroit, Texas
Klondike, Texas
Memphis, Texas
Miami, Texas
Nevada, Texas
New York, Texas
Pasadena, Texas
Pittsburgh, Texas
Reno, Texas
Santa Fe, Texas
Tennessee Colony, Texas
Texas City, Texas

**The solar system comes to Texas:**
Earth, Texas
Mars, Texas
Venus, Texas

**Historical Texas:**
Alamo, Texas
Goliad, Texas
Gun Barrel City, Texas
Robert Lee, Texas
Santa Anna, Texas

**By the Texas fireplace:**
Blanket, Texas
Winters, Texas

**For the ungrowed Texans:**
Elmo, Texas
Kermit, Texas
Nemo, Texas
Sylvester, Texas
Tarzan, Texas
Winnie, Texas

**Names that don't fit but are too fun to miss:**
Baby Head, Texas
Bee House, Texas
Best, Texas
Veribest, Texas
Bigfoot, Texas
Cactus,Texas
Cut and Shoot, Texas
Dime Box, Texas
Old Dime Box, Texas
Ding Dong, Texas
Farewell, Texas
Frognot, Texas
Gun Barrel City, Texas
Hogeye, Texas
Hoop And Holler, Texas
Jot 'Em Down, Texas
Kickapoo, Texas
Knott, Texas (if not Texas, what is it?)
Muleshoe, Texas
Notrees, Texas
Skeeterville, Texas
Telephone, Texas
Telegraph, Texas
Twitty, Texas (wonder if they could get a corporate sponsorship if they renamed the town Twitter)
Uncertain, Texas

Whiteface, Texas
And you don't need to go above the Mason-Dixon line to see
Whitehouse, Texas

Reklaw, Texas, got its name because the name the citizens
wanted, Walker, was already taken. So they flipped it. The
same thinking created the name Sacul (Lucas).

By the way, if you're in Dalhart, Texas, the state capital in
Austin is farther away than the state capitals in New Mexico,
Colorado, Wyoming, Kansas, and Oklahoma.

If you're driving down Route 66, 220 miles out of
Oklahoma City and 42 miles west of Amarillo, and see a
concrete cross that's 190 feet tall, you're in Groom, Texas.

## *The Eiffel Tower in Paris – Texas*

The good folks of Paris, Texas, got tired of tourists asking
where the Eiffel Tower was, so they built one in 1995. Boiler
Makers Local #902 built it right next to the Love Civic Center.
This isn't the tallest Eiffel Tower replica in the country (beaten
handily by a 540 foot tall version built in Las Vegas in 1999),
but it makes more sense than most of them since it's in Paris
(Texas).

For the Texas part, the good folks of Paris, Texas, added a
big red cowboy hat to the top of their Eiffel Tower in 1998.
You can't climb it, but you get see it for free. And the locals
speak the right language and are polite, two more advantages to
the Eiffel Tower in Paris (Texas).

An account from the Texas panhandle in 1882, from the
town and paper *Mobeetie*, should give pause at the weather in
Texas.

"John Pimble's mule, Anastasia, died last week. Anastasia
was standing in a field of popping corn, which, due to the heat,
began popping and covered the ground to a depth of three feet.

The mule, thinking the popcorn was snow, froze to death."

C. W. Post, the Post of Post Cereals, visited the Texas Panhandle in 1906. The famous Texas weather got to him, as it gets to many.

"At nine o'clock Sunday morning the day was as pretty as one could care for. At nine fifteen I had suspicions that I was in search of the North Pole."

Must have been one of those famous "blue northers" that whistle down from Canada to Texas in a matter of minutes. You can see the blue wall of the norther headed your way, and there's nothing you can do. Well, you can trade your shorts and t-shirt for long johns and a parka. In fact, that's the smartest thing to do when that blue wall of weather heads your way.

### The Forbidden City Near Houston

The original Forbidden City was built between 1406 and 1420 in the middle of Beijing, China, but a 1/20th scale copy can be seen in Forbidden Gardens in Katy, Texas. Replicas include the Terra Cotta Army, the Chinese Forbidden City including the palace and gardens, the Summer Palace, the Weapons Room, the Architecture Room, and tiny sculptured people.

Ira Poon, a Seattle native, built the museum in 1997 in Houston because of the large Asian population and low land prices. Next time you're near Houston, check out 2,000 years of Chinese history on the 40-acre Forbidden Gardens site (www.forbidden-gardens.com).

### The Expensive Hole in the Dallas Donut

Officially, Highland Park is an enclave of Dallas, in that the town is entirely contained within the boundaries of another territory. Think of Highland Park as the hole of a donut, and Dallas is the donut. But in this case, the donut hole is worth far more than the donut itself.

Do you prefer the spelling doughnut? So do we, but shops usually can't afford to buy all those letters for their signs, so donut has become the more or less official spelling. Those who believe this is another example of the decline of modern civilization can argue amongst yourselves.

Fried doughy treat discussions notwithstanding, Highland Park shares a strong kinship with Beverly Hills, California. Actually, several kinships, because both are extremely expensive to live in and are therefore full of rich folks. They were also both planned by a landscape architect named Wilbur David Cook.

Highland Park started when a group of investors from Philadelphia came down in 1889 and bought 1,326 acres of undeveloped land about four miles north of downtown Dallas for $500,000. That's an average of $377 per acre, less than the cost of getting the carpets cleaned in the guesthouse of one of the expensive homes (nee mansions) in Highland Park today. If you invent a time machine, real estate bargains are everywhere.

> *It's so beautiful in Texas in the winter, heaven doesn't interest them, and so hot in the summer, hell doesn't scare them.*
>
> *– Texas preacher's lament*

Of course, life tends to mess up plans. The Panic of 1893 brought an end to Philadelphia Place, as the future Highland Park area was called at the time. However, Dallas folks liked to picnic at the lake the developers built before all their money and grand plans drowned.

John Armstrong came in and bought the Philadelphia Place land in 1906. He had been in development earlier, then sold out to get into meatpacking, then sold that to get back into development. Hard to imagine two disciplines farther apart than land development and meatpacking, but Armstrong seemed to enjoy going back and forth.

Luckily, Armstrong refrained from using any cutesy animal part names (would you want to live on Spleen Terrace?) and named the area Highland Park because the slight elevation gave the area a good look at downtown Dallas. Besides the aforementioned Wilbur David Cook from Beverly Hills, Armstrong and his partners brought in local planner George E. Kessler, who did much of the design for downtown Dallas and all of Fair Park.

Highland Park asked Dallas to annex them in 1913, but Dallas refused. And then Dallas refused to annex them again after a couple years of wrangling. Then Dallas decided they really, really wanted Highland Park, and started a battle to annex them that lasted until 1945, when Highland Park finally made it clear they wanted to stay independent. If nothing else, this says Highland Park folks are above average thinkers and were plenty smart enough to avoid being sucked into the Dallas bog.

By 1933 Highland Park had 12 businesses and 8,422 residents. Being an enclave meant no room to expand, and the population in 2000 had only grown to 8,842. The town would love to expand their schools, but there's no room. Tearing down a $3 million home for a school parking lot expansion just seems wrong. And you can't use eminent domain on rich people, because they can afford their own legal team to fight back.

> *The King Ranch in South Texas is larger than the state of Rhode Island.*

Highland Park borders another enclave, University Park, to the north. University Park is larger than Highland Park (23,324 residents in 2000). SMU (Southern Methodist University) is in University Park, but quite close to Highland Park.

133

University Park started as a few homes around SMU in 1915. Hard to believe today, but the area was pretty rural at the time. Early photos of SMU show nothing around but empty fields. In 1924 UP asked HP to annex them, but HP refused because the cost of running utilities was too high. Dallas also refused to annex them.

So University Park organized themselves, starting in 1924, and by 1945 had over 20,000 residents. Nearly double the size of Highland Park (2,350 acres versus 1,326), University Park is also blocked from any expansion since they are also an enclave of Dallas.

HP and UP, the Park Cities, have much in common. Depending on which list you read, Highland Park is about the fourth richest city in Texas, and University Park is between seventh and twelfth. Those are great neighborhoods, just like the Park Cities themselves.

# Weapons
# and
# War

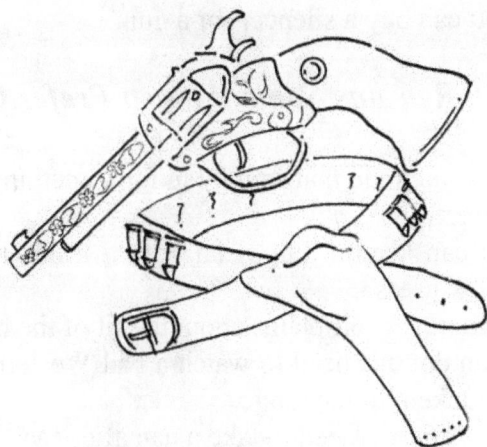

## Top 10 Reasons Some Men Prefer Guns Over Women

10. You can trade an old .44 for a new .22, or maybe two of them.
9. You can keep one gun at home and use another when you're on the road.
8. If you admire a friend's gun, he'll let you try it yourself a few times.
7. Your primary gun doesn't mind if you have a backup gun, and vice versa.
6. A gun doesn't need much closet space.
5. Guns function normally every day of the month.
4. A gun doesn't ask, "Does this holster make me look fat?"
3. A gun doesn't mind if you go to sleep after you use it.
2. Your gun will stay with you even when you run out of bullets.

And the Number One Reason some men favor a gun over a woman is...

1. You can buy a silencer for a gun.

## Top 10 Reasons Some Women Prefer Guns Over Men

10. You can trade that snubby in for something larger and more powerful.
9, You can keep a gun clean with a little Hoppe's and some elbow grease.
8. A gun never complains about the fit of the holster.
7. A gun doesn't need to watch a bad Western on video before you take it to the range.
6. A gun doesn't need to take a nap after each shot.
5. You can carry a gun in your pants all day without it becoming a problem.

4. A gun doesn't complain when you spend more than 15 minutes at the range.

3. Noxious gas emissions can be controlled.

2. A gun doesn't call you a tease if you load it but don't let it shoot.

And the Number One Reason some women favor a gun over a man is...

1. A gun will shoot, reload quickly, and shoot again just as powerfully. Then keep performing again and again and again until YOU'RE tired.

> *I only use my gun whenever kindness fails.*
> *— Robert Earl Keen, singer and songwriter*

## Hunters Not All There

Nearly 40 years ago, some locals in Olney Texas were talking about the right types of guns for hunters missing an arm to use during dove season. Other folks in the drugstore started listening, and the two old friends, as Texans sometimes do, started exaggerating a bit to entertain the eavesdroppers. Soon the friends decided a one-armed bird hunt would be a great thing, since there were six people missing an arm in the town of 3,300. They organized the hunt, and another 10 or 11 out-of-towners came to turn the crazy idea into a social event.

That social event continues to this day, and the number of hunters missing one or more appendage now reaches almost 100. During the event, the odd sight is seeing someone with all their arms and legs. Many folks come from all over the country to visit with others who understand their daily life issues far better than anyone else.

For the record, the most popular recipe for the doves is to stuff them with jalapenos and wrap them in bacon. Good eatin' with good friends, even if many of them can't use a knife and fork at the same time.

## Dead Man's Hole

Can a hole be a weapon? It can when used during a war.

Dead Man's Hole, in a pasture in Marble Falls in southern Burnet County, was discovered in 1821. Geologists expect the hole was caused by natural gas pressure, and for many years no one had the courage to fully investigate the depths of the hole for fear of an explosion.

This fear didn't stop locals, during the War of Northern Aggression, from tossing Union sympathizers down into the hole. Oral historians say 17 people were tossed down the hole during the war and Reconstruction (darn carpetbaggers). No, they weren't cruel enough to just throw them in. They hung them first from a branch over the hole. When the bodies were cut loose, gravity handled disposal.

In 1951 some brave souls from the University of Texas spelunked down the hole. While only seven feet wide at the top, it spread out to about 160 feet at the bottom. One section of the bottom went straight back for about 15 feet, while the other section had a downward slope of about 45 degrees for thirty more feet.

Don't get any ideas. The tree is gone, and the hole entrance is now covered by a steel grate. It seems tossing people down a hole offends modern sensibilities.

## USS Texas

In 1914, the most powerful weapon in the world was named Texas, or, more accurately, the battleship *USS Texas*. Launched on May 18, 1912, and commissioned in 1914, the *USS Texas* served in both World War I and World War II. She was the first with mounted anti-aircraft guns, pretty quick considering the Wright Brothers made their first flight only nine years before the USS *Texas* was launched. This vessel served as the flagship for the bombardment group supporting the Omaha Beach landings on D-Day.

You can see the *USS Texas* yourself moored beside the San Jacinto Monument just off the Houston ship channel. Currently recommissioned though not on active duty, the *USS Texas* is the flagship of the Texas Navy.

Somewhere near the border of Afghanistan and Pakistan, a large number of Taliban soldiers were moving from one secret base to another. From just over the hill, they heard a voice with a twang call out, "One Texas soldier is better than ten stinkin' Taliban soldiers."

The Taliban cleric/general in charge immediately ordered the closest 10 soldiers to check behind the hill. The men charged over the hill, yelling and screaming, only to be met with yelling in return as well as multiple gunshots. After a moment, the gunshots stopped and the echoes bounced off nearby hills and faded away.

"That was pathetic," yelled the same voice from behind the hill. "One Texan is better than one hundred stinkin' Taliban."

Angrily, the Taliban leader ordered his best squad over the hill to kill the Texan. Better trained than the first group, the Taliban squad moved briskly but quietly to the top of the hill, and then started firing as they went over the top and out of sight.

More gunshots echoed through the area, mixed with the screams of dying soldiers. After five minutes the gunfire and screaming stopped.

"Y'all should be ashamed to call yourselves soldiers," came the voice from over the hill. "One Texan is better'n one thousand worthless stinkin' Taliban."

The Taliban leader ordered the best of his remaining squads to find and silence the insolent infidel Texan. As the men charged over the hill, the remaining troops fired mortars and tank shells over the hill in support.

For 45 minutes the battle raged, as gunfire, stray bullets, and screams came from behind the hill. Silence descended on the area as the echoes of war rang through the valley.

One wounded Taliban soldier staggered over the hill, bleeding from multiple wounds and barely able to walk. He fell, and then crawled the rest of the way to the commander, who knelt low to hear his final words.

"Don't send any more men, your Excellency," whispered the dying Taliban soldier. "It's a trap. There are actually two Texans."

## *The Gonzalez Cannon*

Not to be confused with the Pachelbel Kanon, a lovely piece of music, the Gonzalez cannon helped start the Texas revolution and the separation from Mexico. Pretty good for a six-pound brass (although one account says iron) cannon, don't you think?

Settlers in the Gonzalez area requested a cannon to use when defending themselves from Indian attacks. A Mr. Green DeWitt, who got an empresario land grant from the Mexican government and promptly named the area DeWitt (those Kentucky boys have an ego, don't they?), requested a cannon on January 1, 1831. By March 10, the cannon arrived. Amazing that before telephones and email, the government worked faster than it does now in many cases. Just try ordering a cannon today from a government official and see how long it takes.

Not much was said about the cannon for the next four and a half years, so we can assume it was mounted on one of the two blockhouses that protected the city of Gonzalez. But in September 1835, a corporal and five soldiers came from Mexico to take the cannon back.

It seems the Mexicans thought the cannon was on loan, while the Texians thought the cannon was a gift. Before lawyers or a legal arbitration service could be called, the Texians turned the Mexican soldiers into prisoners and buried the cannon in a peach orchard. Unfortunately, the "sleep with the peaches" threat didn't catch on as well as the Mafia's later "sleep with the fishes," but it provided better shade.

Not surprisingly, the Mexican military wasn't thrilled that neither the cannon nor the soldiers returned. While the Mexicans were organizing a larger force of about 100 men to retrieve said cannon, the Texians gathered together about 30 seasoned Indian fighters. The Texians unburied the cannon, mounted it on a pair of cartwheels, and made ready for the Mexican soldiers to come and try to get the cannon.

When the two groups faced off on October 2, 1835, the Mexicans demanded the return of the cannon. The Texian "Army of the People" pointed 200 yards behind them and said, "come and take it." Odd that a chant at the sophistication level of a second grade school yard made it into Texas history, but stranger things of happened (see the Pig War, for example).

Texian womenfolk, not to be left out, quickly sewed a flag for the standoff. A black cannon stood in the middle of a white flag, with the words, "Come and Take It" above and below the artillery piece. Officially, the first flag of the Texas Revolution sounds like a school kid's dare, but those were simpler times.

Using the cannon and the Army of the People, the Texians took over Goliad and later San Antonio. The Gonzalez Cannon was used in the Battle of the Alamo, and was likely melted down by the Mexican army after the battle.

## Nuclear Hands Up

A great one for the "only in Texas" file: two duck hunters near Amarillo scared a nuclear weapons plant shut. This story was reported around Texas, the US, and even in England. Amazing how fierce Texas duck hunters can be.

According to the *London Telegraph* story on January 15, 2010, Carson County Sheriff Tam Terry said, "Somebody saw some armed individuals dressed in camouflage clothing exiting the vicinity of the plant." This caused such an alarm the plant was locked down. The Pantex plant stores, repairs, and decommissions nuclear weapons for the U.S. government, so security tends to be a bit tight there.

However, one might expect the might of the U.S. military could stand firm against two duck hunters. But then again, these were Texas duck hunters.

Luckily for the Pantex guards, the duck hunters surrendered without a fight because they weren't attacking, just looking for ducks. After some identity verification and a check that the hunters didn't have a record for attacking nuclear facilities, everyone parted friends and the boys went elsewhere looking for their duck dinner.

But the big question is this: as dry as Amarillo is, they still have ducks?

## *The Twin Sisters*

Two cannons nicknamed the Twin Sisters provided almost all the artillery for the Republic of Texas Army as they fought Santa Anna. The Texas Hysterical Society happily bestows the label of Honorary Texan on the Twin Sisters. Well, we would if we could find them.

A gift from the good people of Cincinnati to the upstarts trying to free Texas from Mexico, the Twin Sisters were cast by the Greenwood and Webb foundry in Cincinnati and shipped down the Mississippi in 1836. They arrived in New Orleans on March 16 and were shipped over to Galveston via the *Pennsylvania*, arriving in early April.

The two six pounders got their name during their presentation to the good people of Texas. Dr. Charles Rice, moving to Texas with his family, somehow managed to get his twin daughters Elizabeth and Eleanor to present the cannons to the Texas delegation. Perhaps he was auditioning the family for a reality TV show, and hoped twin guns and twin girls would catch the eye of a Hollywood producer.

Twins of girls and guns caught the eye of the crowd, and someone mentioned there were two twins in the dedications. From that time on, the two cannon were called the Twin Sisters. The Rice girls, from that time on, were still called Elizabeth and Eleanor, and they didn't get a reality show contract, even though their proposed title, *The Texas Shore*, seemed appropriate for the situation.

The Twin Sisters (cannons) just about saved the day during the Battle of San Jacinto, surprising and confusing Mexican troops by firing from over 200 yards away. Unfortunately, the Texans were out of real ammunition, and stuffed the guns with horseshoes, broken glass, and musket balls.

During their leave after the Revolution, the Twin Sisters (cannons) stayed in Austin. They were fired for the fifth anniversary of the Battle of San Jacinto, which should have been nicely nostalgic for them. They also fired at the moment Sam Houston kissed the Bible during his swearing in as president of the Republic of Texas.

During the "merger" between Texas and the United States, all weapons and various items (like the Navy) related to public defense were ceded to the United States. The Twins almost got a reprieve as being more relics of a glorious past than modern weapons of war, but alas, they went to an armory in Baton Rouge.

As the secession talks heated up in 1860, Texan military folks decided the Twin Sisters might be useful. George Williamson, commissioner for Louisiana to the state of Texas, discovered them in a foundry before they were melted for scrap. The nice state to the east then appropriated some money to restore the Twin Sisters to functioning order and returned them to Texas.

The Twin Sisters made an appearance at the Battle of Galveston on New Year's Day, 1863. Alongside the guns were the girls Elizabeth and Eleanor Rice, auditioning for a new reality TV show called *The Galveston Shore*. Alas, again the network suits didn't approve, and the girls faded back into historical obscurity.

Alas again, for the guns also faded into obscurity. The last credible sighting of the Twin Sisters was in Market Square in Houston on July 30, 1865. Legend says some Texas Confederate soldiers buried them somewhere in Houston to keep them out of Yankee hands, but then forgot where they put them. If you can find them, you will solve one of the big mysteries left over from early Texas.

## *Roosevelt on Rangers*

Teddy Roosevelt recruited some Texans for his Rough Riders, and had this to say about them in 1898.

"We drew a great many recruits from Texas; and from nowhere did we get a higher average, for many of them had served in that famous body of frontier fighters, the Texas Rangers...They were splendid shots, horsemen, and trailers. They were accustomed to living in the open, to enduring great fatigue and hardship, and to encountering all kinds of danger."

Let the record show the great Teddy was referring to real Texas Rangers, not the baseball team that usually teases fans in the Dallas-Fort Worth area every year by winning early in the season, then fading faster than New Year's Resolutions after the All Star break. Good news, finally, as the Rangers got to the 2010 World Series. They lost to the San Francisco Giants, but they did have the pleasure of beating the New York Yankees in the playoffs.

An old cowboy went to an Indian celebration, and sought out the medicine man. "Can you remove a curse I've been living with for the last thirty-seven years?"

The medicine man looked him up and down, then asked, "Can you tell me the exact words that were used to curse you?"

"I now pronounce you man and wife."

The lovely Mrs. Patterson, a seventh-generation Texan, rolled through a stop sign just a bit too quickly one day. A police officer pulled her over.

Mrs. Patterson handed him her driver's license, insurance card, and concealed handgun license.

"Are you carrying today, ma'am?" asked the officer.

"I carry every day."

"Can you tell me what you have on you today, ma'am?"

Mrs. Patterson started counting on her fingers. "Well, there's a 9mm semi-auto in my purse, and a .357 in the glove box."

"Okay," said the officer. "Anything else?"

"Wait, I have a .22 derringer in my right boot."

"Okay, that's quite a bit."

"And in the trunk there's an AR15 and a 12 gauge pump shotgun with a pistol grip. That's about it."

"Mrs. Patterson, are you on your way home from the firing range?"

"Nope."

"Well then, what exactly are you afraid of?" asked the officer.

"Not a damn thing, young man, not a damn thing."

# Animals

## *Killer Bee Capital of the World*

Yes, that's the entomological nickname for Hidalgo, down in South Texas. In fact, it's so far down in South Texas it's almost the southern-most town in the state. Smack against the border with Mexico, Hidalgo is an old town with some history.

Recent history looms large in the guise of a 21 foot long Killer Bee Statue in front of the Public Library. The first Africanized killer bee found in the U. S. appeared in Hidalgo on October 15, 1990. Since not much else happens in Hidalgo, the city put up the statue and declared itself the Killer Bee Capital of the World.

So far as we can tell, this is the largest killer bee monument anywhere (hey, it is Texas after all). People love to have their picture made with the bee, and come from a long way, as do reporters from places like the *Oprah Winfrey Show* and *The Wall Street Journal*.

Moving fast, the statue was unveiled to the public on December 6, 1992. That's just two years after the first killer bee colonies were found. Rarely does city government move so quickly, but killer bees wait for no man, or committee.

During a campout in the Texas Hill Country, a young Boy Scout woke to find himself being flown out of his tent by four mosquitoes, each grabbing one corner of his sleeping bag.

"Should we take him back home?" asked one mosquito.

"No," answered another. "If we do, one of the big ones might take him away from us."

## *Cockroach Hall of Fame*

Michael Bohdan, exterminator, got bitten by the TV bug when he was the Bug Man on some episodes of the famous *Mr. Peppermint* show (Jerry Haynes, aka Mr. Peppermint, presided over a kids show on local Dallas TV from 1961 to 1996). He ran a Cockroach Costume Contest for Combat (the bug spray

148

folks) in the 1980s, then kept some of the entrants after the event and started a museum. Yes, the Cockroach Hall of Fame Museum is in Plano, a suburb north of Dallas.

Officially The Pest Shop (pestshop.com), the museum is in the front, and Bohdan's exterminator business lives in the back. Bring your bugs to Bohdan, and he'll sell you the safest and most effective products to help rid you of your pests.

Bohdan's fully costumed roaches include:

Liberoache

Ross Peroach

Marilyn Monroach (with white billowy skirt above a grate)

He had a roach Last Supper, including 12 tiny plates in front of each roach. Sadly, someone stole it. Bad way to treat the former Regional Director of the Texas Pest Control Association.

"People hate bugs, but when they're dressed up in a tutu, they're not so bad," says Bohdan. Of course, dressing up dead bugs is easier than getting the clothes on the live ones.

### Bobby Joe Strikes Again

Bobby Joe was leaving Lake Ray Hubbard when a Game Warden asked to see his fishing license. While without a license, Bobby Joe still had his wits, so he told the officer, "Oh, you think I caught these fish? No sir, officer, I did not. These are pet fish."

"You got live fish in a bucket, so you were fishing," said the warden.

"No sir. These are pets. But they get frustrated by the small tank I have at home, so every couple of days I bring'em down here to run free a bit, like taking your dog to the dog park. I dump them into the water, let them swim around for a few minutes, then whistle. They know what means it's time to go home, so they come and jump in the bucket."

"Sorry, but you were fishing."

Bobby Joe led the warden back to the lake. "If you don't

believe me, then watch," he said as he threw the fish into the lake.

"Ok, now whistle and get your pet fish back," said the game warden.

Bobby Joe, scratching his head thoughtfully, looked at the warden. "What fish?"

## *Reveille*

Reveille, now always a female full-blooded Collie, is the official mascot of Texas A&M University. This tradition started back in January 1931.

Some members of the Aggie band were coming home late one night from a party in a nearby city, when they accidentally hit a small black and white stray mutt. Surely there were no adult beverages involved, although the group thought the best thing to do was to bring the injured dog and hide her in their dorm room. They planned to take her to the veterinarian school (A&M has one of the best in the country) in the morning and thereby avoid getting caught.

Alas, the dog heard the traditional bugle call alarm clock (A&M was a strongly military school at the time) and started barking. The dog-hiding students got caught, but they did give the dog a name: Reveille. Even better, they kept from getting themselves deeper into trouble by convincing the Powers That Be to make Reveille a band mascot.

Being band students, the group arranged for Reveille to lead the band onto the field during the first football game in the fall for their half time show. During the game, she wore a jacket with A&M colors and roamed the sideline, suggesting plays to the coaches.

So many A&M graduates served with distinction in the armed forces that the U.S. Army paid them the honor of giving Reveille the rank of Cadet General in 1944. It's an honor to the students to have them all be outranked by the dog? It is at A&M.

After Reveille I died later that year, she was buried at the north entrance of Kyle Field, the football stadium, in a formal military funeral. This location was chosen so she could always see the scoreboard and rejoice as the Aggies outscored their opponents. Oh, well, it was a nice thought. Too bad the football team didn't win every game for Reveille's sake.

The next couple of years, the school tried a variety of other mascots, but Tripod, Spot, and Ranger didn't work out. In 1952, a donated Shetland Sheepdog was officially designated Reveille II, the unofficial school mascot. The Fightin' Texas Aggie Band cared for her for a couple of years, but she was found wandering loose on campus in 1954. The school refused to pay for her care, so one student, Sam Netterville, convinced the Student Senate to pass a resolution ordering his unit, A Quartermaster Company, to provide for the dog.

Young Sam took Reveille II everywhere with him, including classes. Smart boy, because Shelties are cute little chick magnets. The tradition to always escort Reveille took hold because of young Sam. Called "Miss Rev," the dog marched with the Aggie Band during football games.

Some other traditions:

If Reveille decides to sleep on a student's bed, that student must sleep on the floor.

All cadets address Reveille as "Miss Rev, ma'am."

If she is in class, and barks while the professor is actually teaching, class must be dismissed immediately. (This rule is sometimes ignored by long-winded professors).

Reveille III was the first full-blooded collie chosen as the mascot. All Reveilles since her have also been collies. Reveille IV had over 10,000 mourners at her funeral on April 9, 1989. Either they really love their mascots at A&M, or a bunch of kids wanted out of class.

The school "auditioned" over 2,000 puppies before finding exactly the right Reveille V. TCU refused her entrance into their stadium in 1987 citing some stupid rule about disallowing live mascots at home games. Really bad sportsmanship, TCU. Bad PR move as well. Just about everybody loves Reveille, even other schools. She's class all the way, although Reveille V was a bit of a scamp and liked to steal erasers off the chalkboards during classes. How can you yell "bad dog" at the Cadet General?

Reveille VI was stolen in 1993 by a University of Texas at Austin student during the winter break. Evidently, her escort cadet left her in the back yard at his parent's home in Dallas. Stupid, young cadet, stupid. Up to that time. Reveille was the only mascot in the Southwest Conference that hadn't been stolen.

Following military protocol, A&M stonewalled and refused to admit Reveille VI was missing. The thief blew that cover-up when he left her tied to a sign near Lake Travis in Austin, and called the police. Should have called the TV stations, but they found out anyway.

Reveille's student cadet, a sophomore in Company E-2, must take her everywhere, including classes (probably poking the poor dog to get her to bark and stop the class). When the cadet goes on dates, Reveille must go as chaperone.

How serious do they take Reveille at Texas A&M? Deadly. In 1997, when the school expanded the football stadium, they moved the resting places of all the Reveilles from the north entrance so a new spot across the street. People became outraged, because from their new resting place, the dogs could no longer see the scoreboard. So the school built a small scoreboard on the side of the stadium and named it the Reveille Scoreboard.

## Ships of the Desert

In 1836, most experts believed the west was full of desert and darn near uninhabitable (many in Los Angeles today agree). What animals do well carrying people and cargo in the desert? Camels, of course, the original four wheel drive mammals. So in 1855, when the U.S. War Department wanted to test camels in lieu of horses and mules, they went to North Africa, bought 33 camels (one calf was born en route), then took them to Texas. Of course! Where else but Texas to test some camels?

The camels worked great, at least for their official duties. They carried as much as 600 pounds of equipment, went seemingly forever without needing water, and ate any ragged vegetation they could find. A trip through the unexplored Big Bend area proved they could be useful. The Army ordered another 41 more not long after.

Groups went from Texas all the way to California. During the Civil War, a Confederate spy and Texas lawyer, Bethel Coopwood, captured 14 camels and two Egyptian drivers, and brought them back to Texas.

Useful, but not great. Unlike the sand of North Africa, much of the Texas desert was rocky, and that hurt the camels' feet. Horses were scared of the camels, so the military men and their love of neat formations suffered badly. Plus, camels stink something fierce, are ornery, and will bite when given a chance.

By 1866 the Army decided that mules, as bad as they were, beat camels. The Army gave up on their camel capers, and sold the ones they had left at auction. Coopwood, interestingly, bought 66 of them. Some were sold in California, and others escaped to wander around Texas for a few more years.

### Let's Go Batty

As in Mexican free-tailed bats, tens of thousands of which migrate to Austin every year starting around March, and stay until cold fronts drive them back to Mexico in November. Estimates on the number of bats range up to 1.5 million, making it the largest known urban bat colony in the world. Tourists and bat-fans love to watch the swarm zoom away from the Congress Avenue Bridge at sunset. The flock is so large it appears on weather radar screens.

The bats appeared after the bridge, now named for popular governor Ann W. Richards, was renovated in 1980. It appears the engineers inadvertently created a wonderful bat habitat. Long horizontal grooves, openings well suited for baby bat nurseries, run the length of the bridge. Since roosting densities are up to 500 babies per square foot, a long bridge can hold a bunch of baby bats.

Tourists love the bats, and local business people estimate the bats draw about $10 million per year in visitor revenue. Thousands line up to watch the flock fly out searching for the estimated 20,000 pounds of flying insect pests like mosquitoes they eat every night.

These bats are pretty cool if you like flying mammals. A Mexican free-tailed bat, built for speed with short fur and long narrow wings, can go as fast as 60mph (with a friendly tail wind). They have been observed flying up to 10,000 feet high and 100 miles from their nest.

Could the bridge engineers have cleverly renovated the bridge in such a way to encourage the bats, and therefore the tourists? Nah. Governments rarely think that far ahead. If they had tried such a thing, committees would have ruined the design to the point Austin would have the largest urban skunk population. Since the state government hosts politicians and draws lobbyists like flies (can we get the bats to attack them?), Austin suffers enough. Enjoy the bats.

## The Mustangs of Las Colinas

It's horses and it's big, so it must be Texas.

The world's largest equestrian (fancy name for horse) statue is, where else, in Texas. Oddly, the statue installation (there are nine wild mustangs running across a stream) is part of one of the premier business parks in Texas, Las Colinas. But they were put there for all the right reasons: it's Texas, they're big, and they're mustangs.

Ben H. Carpenter's official story of the Las Colinas development is that he had a "vision to transform his family's ranch, fondly named El Ranchito de Las Colinas, meaning the Little Ranch of the Hills, into a world class development." Hence the name Las Colinas for the huge business and residential development.

We at the Texas Hysterical Society can smell revisionist history as pungent as equestrian waste. The story at the time was that the Carpenter family's land was too lousy for growing anything except weeds, but was conveniently located near the new DFW International Airport. How bad is the land? Stories abounded in the early days of horrible foundation problems in some buildings, but things seem to have stabilized since then (or the rumor mill is tired of the same old story).

Be that as it may, Carpenter's plan to make a statement by putting in the mustangs was genius. He commissioned sculptor Robert Glen in 1976 to create the installation, asking that they be proportioned to be viewed and enjoyed from any angle. Glen spent a year studying mustangs and the history of these magnificent animals (or he was busy with ongoing work), and scale models led to larger models done in plasticine, a material easier to work with in detail than clay. Then they were cast with fiberglass and resin to create molds ready for casting full metal statues.

The Morris Singer Foundry outside London has cast many famous sculptures, including the lions in Trafalgar Square. Casting was finished by late 1981, but plenty of work remained. On September 25th, 1984, the statue was opened to the public. Each mustang is one and a half times bigger than life size, and weighs about two tons.

If you have a chance when leaving the DFW International Airport, take a detour to Las Colinas and Williams Square, and take a few minutes to check out the mustangs at 5205 N. O'Conner Drive. You'll feel freer the rest of your day.

There are more tigers in Texas than in India. Of course, in India they are wild, hunted, and endangered. In Texas, they are owned by private individuals, which is completely legal in Texas. You can have a tiger in your yard just like you can have a dog, but your mailman will be much more nervous.

Tighter and tighter restrictions on large predators like tigers are ending the "tiger on the porch" lifestyle favored by some. Curse that powerful mailman lobby.

Every Texan knows that when you have young kids, you need at least one dog. Sure, there are plenty of life lessons about unconditional love and responsibility for our four-legged friends, but more important, the dog keeps the kitchen and dining area floors clean. Parents without a dog in the house are advised to keep not a broom handy to clean the floor but a snow shovel.

## A Texan Down Under

A successful and somewhat boastful Texas rancher took his lovely wife on a trip to Australia one winter, for two reasons: to enjoy summer Down Under, and because it was cheaper to take her on an international trip than let her go to Neiman-Marcus again.

While there, the rancher wanted to do a little business, of course. He arranged a spa day for his wife in Sydney, and he went to visit a couple of ranches.

The Australian rancher sat on the porch and waved his hands toward the ranch. "This ranch runs for forty kilometers in every direction."

"Hmm," said the Texan, "that's only about twenty five miles. My ranch in Texas is much bigger than that."

The Australian walked his guest over to the edge of a cattle pen. "These are my prize steers. The one with the white blaze won grand prize at last year's rodeo."

"Hmm," said the Texan, "my steers about twice that big.

Hell, the horns on my longhorns are almost as big as some of your cows."

As the two walked back toward one of the barns, a troop of kangaroos hopped by. The Texan stopped and stared, mouth wide open.

"What's the matter, mate?" asked the Australian. "Are those bigger than your Texas grasshoppers?"

## *How to Find Bass Bait*

Bobby Joe went fishing one fine afternoon, and had just about run out of worms when a cottonmouth snake swam by with a frog in his mouth. Frogs make good bass bait.

Knowing the snake couldn't bite him with a mouth full of frog, Bobby Joe reached out into the water and grabbed the cottonmouth right behind his head. He pulled the snake into the boat then pulled the frog loose and dropped it into his bait bucket.

That meant Bobby Joe now held a cottonmouth that not only had his mouth free for business, but was angry at losing the frog. How to get rid of the snake? If he threw him, the snake could catch his hand during the throw.

Desperate, Bobby Joe pulled out his lunch, a bottle of Jack Daniels whiskey. Careful not to spill any more than necessary, Bobby Joe poured a bit of the whiskey into the snake's mouth. The snake's eyes rolled back, he shuddered three times, then went limp. Bobby Joe carefully put the snake back in the water and was relieved to see the snake wake up and swim away in a somewhat lopsided, staggering manner.

Ten minutes later, Bobby Joe heard a knock on the side of the boat. The cottonmouth was back, and he had two frogs.

# Arts
# and
# Society

## *A Texas-based H. L. Mencken*

William Cowper Brann followed the popular joke bumper sticker of "I wasn't born in Texas, but I got here as fast as I could." In Brann's case, Texas meant Waco in 1895, slightly before bumper stickers. There he started a monthly paper called *Iconoclast* that at one time had over 100,000 subscribers throughout Texas and the rest of the United States. He published over a million words in forty monthly issues until he was shot in the back in downtown Waco.

As a scathing satirist and social commentator, Brann belongs on the same honored shelf as Ambrose Bierce and H. L. Mencken, but alas, few remember him. Shame. Anyone who can satirize Baptists in Waco to the point he gets jumped by "God fearin' men," including a judge on the board of Baylor University, and beaten to the point of a month long recuperation, earned his Texas honors the hard way, especially since he didn't leave town as his attackers ordered.

Here's how Brann responded after his beating: "I walk the streets of Waco day by day, and I walk them alone. Let these cur-ristians shoot me in the back if they dare, then plead that damning lie as excuse for their craven cowardice."

The particular lie Brann referred to? That he had slandered Southern women, which of course was ridiculous. Who had he really "slandered" on a regular basis? The Baptist Church in general, the men running the church, and not to ignore higher education, the men running Baylor University. Baylor was, and is, the college of the Baptist Church much like Notre Dame is the college for Catholics or Brigham Young University "favors" Mormons.

Tom Davis, a supporter of Baylor University, was upset about Brann's frequent skewering of the Baptist college sacred cow status, so he shot Brann in the back "where his suspenders crossed" (the Texas Hysterical Society officially labels Davis a Dishonorable Texan). Brann was able to pull out his own pistol and kill his attacker before he died, a truly Texan death. In fact, he hit Davis with all six shots from his revolver. Even though the cowardly murder happened on one of the main streets of Waco, it screams Texas Wild West.

R.I.P. Mr. Brann, and take some ironic solace in the fact the coward Davis shot you in the back on April Fool's Day, 1898.

### Sign on a Texas country store:
Prom Dresses
Live Bait
Free Puppies
Nowhere but Texas. But really, who wouldn't love to see some puppies at the prom?

### Hoss From DeKalb
The son of Ora Shack and Mary (Davis) Blocker, Dan, was fourteen pounds at his birth on December 10, 1928. Ladies are allowed to stop for a moment and shudder. By age 12, Dan Blocker was over six feet tall and 200 pounds. As a football player at Sul Ross University, he was six feet four inches tall and 275 (or more) pounds.

A teacher bitten with the acting bug, Blocker graduated with a degree in speech and drama, and turned down offers from professional football and boxing to act in summer stock in Boston. After serving in Korea, he came back to Sul Ross and got a masters in dramatic arts.

He taught high school English and drama in Sonora, Texas, before moving to Carlsbad, New Mexico, then on to California. He was working on a Ph.D. when he got his big acting break when cast as Hoss Cartwright on *Bonanza*. Do you realize how rare it is for actors to have any education, much less advanced degrees? Way to go, Hoss.

A director friend wanted to cast him in a movie with the odd name of *Dr. Strangelove*. Stanley Kubrick and co-writer

Terry Southern wanted him for the part of Major T. J. "King" Kong. With the character name, and the famous scene of eventual actor Slim Pickens riding the bomb like a horse, it seems the part was made for Dan Blocker. Alas, his agent said no, as agents too often do, because this character was so different from what Blocker played on *Bonanza*. Hoss missed his chance to make screen history by riding that bomb. Guess Blocker will have to be satisfied with his record of largest baby in Bowie County.

> *The world is a rodeo for your amusement. Hang on and enjoy. Those jerks giving you trouble? Just rodeo clowns. And if you watch long enough, you'll see most of them get gored by an angry bull.*
>
> *– The Old Cowboy*

## Pampa's Music Fence

Pampa, in the panhandle, tends to be a bit breezy at times. Musicians hate it when sheet music blows away. So Russell "Rusty" Neef made some sheet music that will not only stay put in a high wind, but should last for 100 years, even out in the weather.

Go to the M. K. Brown Civic Auditorium in Pampa on N. Hobars Street and take a look at what Neef did in 1993. It took over 400 hours, but the welder built a 150-foot treble clef staff of music in the key of G in 4/4. The tune? "This Land Is Your Land" by Woody Guthrie.

From 1929 to 1937, young Mr. Guthrie lived in Pampa. He arrived when he was 17, so folks like to claim Pampa is where he started actually writing music. That's the kind of oral history one can't really verify, but it makes such a good story you hate to dig deeper and find out the truth.

Neef took on the project in honor of his father, George, who started the welding shop in 1936. Since the song is patriotic, sections of the fence are lit with red, white, and blue lights. When finished, check out the Bound for Glory Park down by the railroad tracks.

> *Money spent on a book is not wasted.*
> *– J'Nell Pate, author*

## Stratford on Avon, er, Odessa

That's Odessa College, a two year junior college in Odessa. Their theater is one of three recreations of Shakespeare's famed stage in the world.

The theater opened in 1968, after a local high school English teacher assigned her students a project building a replica of the Globe Theater. Once finished, some folks had the idea a real Globe Theater would make Odessa even more fun. They got to work, and the Globe opened in 1968.

Sorry, Will, but they also have country music concerts on your stage. Of course, tragedy often looms large in both Shakespeare plays and country music, but no Shakespeare plays mention riding the rails, pickup trucks, or honky tonks. On the other hand, cheating wives and husbands seem to be common to both.

> *I was always proud about being from Texas and, you know, maybe that was part of fearlessness. I love the fact that Texas is so big, but you don't feel small because of that.*
> *– Sissy Spacek, actress*

## The First Thanksgiving

Nope, not Plymouth Rock in a far northern state like Massachusetts, but in far West Texas just across the border from New Mexico. The year? 1598, compared to 1621 for those slowpoke Pilgrims.

Now the site of the small town of San Elizario, in El Paso

County, this part of Texas is what you find first when you get through the mountains by following the Rio Grande. In fact, El Paso is Spanish for "the pass" referring to said mountain passage.

Don Juan de Oriate, Spanish nobleman and conquistador born in Mexico, led 500 colonists and 7,000 head of livestock eastward. When they got through the mountains and found easy access to the Rio Grande they drank the water and celebrated a Thanksgiving Mass with fish, fowl, and deer on April 30, 1598.

Those latecomers, the Pilgrims, had their most famous first Thanksgiving in the fall of 1621, two decades after the one in future Texas. An earlier Thanksgiving in the Virginia colony happened in 1619, still decades after the one in Texas.

## Ace of Clubs House

James Harris Draughton, born in Tennessee in 1843, served as a Confederate lieutenant in the Civil War. After being wounded, captured, and released, he split for Panama to finish out the war. Afterwards, he went through California and Nevada on his way to Cincinnati to attend the Bacon Commercial College. Guess map reading wasn't one of Draughton's strong points, or he might have gotten to Cincinnati a bit more directly. He married and settled in Arkansas in 1870, starting a general store.

During a poker game, the Ace of Clubs won Draughton a big pot. Taking those winnings, Draughton launched a string of successful businesses, and planned his Ace of Clubs House to honor the card that started him on his way.

Hearing that two railroads were about to intersect in an area just across the Texas border, Draughton bought up a bunch of land in what became Texarkana. He moved his store there, and added a lumber business, became the second Mayor of the town (always a good way to make money, legally or not), and became president of the First National Bank (see?). The more money he made, the more heroic his war service, and his rank rose lieutenant (real) to Captain (fudge) to Colonel (so very Southern and respectable).

He started his house in 1885 to help inspire the townspeople to reach for better things. Traveling had given Draughton a bigger view of the world than his fellow citizens, and he wanted to become their "prophet of possibilities."

While that sounds seriously pompous and reeks of a nouveau riche blowhard, he did build one heck of a house. With 12 rooms and every "modern" convenience (it was 1885, after all), the house had two stories and a basement. Highly ornamented and finished with all the finery of southern mansions everywhere, the house stood out as something special then and now. And making Texarkana look special to new businesses and citizens helped Draughton's large real estate holdings.

> *There are no illegitimate children, only illegitimate parents.*
> *— Edna Gladney, Honorary Texan,*
> *child protector of the first order*

But Draughton tired of Texarkana, sold the house in 1887, and moved back to Arkansas. There he started a sawmill and built a town, now called Draughton, in the area. Once again, he did well, getting into the cotton business and helping to start the Shawnee Electric Light and Power Company.

The house is called the Draughton-Moore House of Clubs because Henry Moore, Sr., (not the sculptor, but a successful attorney) bought the place in 1897. It passed to Henry Moore, Jr., when he got married, and he lived there until he died in 1942. His widow Olivia stayed in the house until her death in 1985. She deeded the house to the Texarkana Historical Society, and they have maintained it since.

Opened to the public since 1988, the house's period furnishing and possessions provide a look back to the earlier age. You can tour the house for a surprisingly few dollars

Tuesday through Saturday. Check TexarkanaMuseums.org for details.

> *I have never known anyone from Texas, no matter how far they go or what they do, who isn't proud of being from Texas.*
> *– Van Cliburn, Honorary Texan, world famous pianist*

## Jesus in Cowboy Boots

In the East Texas town of Paris, in the Evergreen Cemetery, lie Willet (1828-1881) and Belinda (1824-1909) Babcock. Willet, born in New York, was quite the successful cabinetmaker, and served on the Board of Directors of the Paris and Great Northern Railroad. Some say he was also the first fire chief in town.

The Babcock memorial includes a pedestal with the engraved particulars, and a statue of Jesus leaning on a cross. Together, the monument is about 15 feet high. Nothing too interesting there, because this is a cemetery and Babcock seemed to have a bit of money.

Looking closer, however, shows that Jesus' left foot is wearing not a sandal but a cowboy boot. The right foot is under his robe, so we can't be sure what's on that one.

No one seems to know any details about the sculptor or commission, which is a shame. Everyone assumes Willet demanded the boot, but we believe otherwise. Belinda Babcock lived 29 more years, and would have likely been the one to make the burial arrangements. Whether she had the statue done at the time of her husband's death or closer to her own demise is a question we would love to have answered. After all, screwy history is our favorite subject.

## Festival for Solenopsis Invicta

That's Fire Ant in the vernacular, sometimes called RIFA

for Red Imported Fire Ant. But RIFA is far too polite a name for the South American ant that hitched a ride to the port of Mobile, Alabama, in the 1930s and have spread everywhere from California to Maryland in the U.S., and to China and Australia as well.

You can hate 'em, but you can't ever completely kill 'em, so Marshall, Texas, a historic East Texas town of over 25,000, decided to make money off of them. Enter the Fire Ant Festival, held the second weekend each October.

The most fun contest seems to the fire ant calling contest. Sure, people all over call for pigs or turkeys, but who but Texans would call for fire ants?

There are three sections to the contest. First, call for food. Second, the alarm call. Finally, the mating call. The fact that ants don't make any sounds, at least that people can hear, pushes the contest participants to focus on creativity rather than accuracy.

If that's not crazy enough for you, enter the fire ant roundup (First prize wins $150). Contestants get an empty plastic milk jug and two hours to round up the most fire ants. They also get huge amounts of sympathy and first aid.

Here's the list of fun events:
- Fire Ant Calling
- Fire Ant Roundup
- 5k Run
- Tour de Fire Ant
- Fire Ant Parade
- Diaper Derby (baby races, not trying to put diapers on ants)
- Rubber Chicken Chunking Contest
- Lip Sync Contest
- Pet Show
- Gurning Contest (British word for Ugly Face Contest)
- Men's Crazy Legs Contest

No offense to our friends in Marshall, but while they have the first (over 25 years) Fire Ant Festival, the latecomers in Ashburn, Georgia, have raised the bar on Fire Ant Festivals. They have a car show, for one. They also have the Miss Fire Ant Pageant. Doesn't that beat the Men's Crazy Leg Contest?

By the way, isn't "invicta" Latin for invincible? That certainly describes the fire ant.

## Tallest Statues

Who's taller, Sam Houston or the giraffe at the Dallas Zoo? Both statues are 67 feet high. Giraffe fans say Sam has an unfair advantage by standing on a 10-foot pedestal. Friends of Sam say the giraffe has six feet of tongue going up just to match their man Sam.

See for yourself, and continue the argument in your own family. Go to the Dallas Zoo for a look at the giraffe. Then head down Interstate 45 toward Houston, and look for Sam's statue two miles south of Huntsville.

FYI, Huntsville loves their Sam Houston. He retired there, and the Sam Houston name gets plastered on just about everything, including a State University (Sam Houston State University).

## Aluminum Siding, 12 Ounces at a Time

Some college students (OK, college boys) like to stack beer cans in their dorm room. For some it's art, for some it's being too lazy to take out the trash, and for some it's giving the finger to "the man" saying the student is officially too young to legally imbibe said beer. But most grow out of this phase. Most never completely cover their house in beer cans. But you can see such a house in Houston, called, appropriately, the Beer Can House.

John Milkovisch, 222 Malone Street in Houston, worked for Southern Pacific Railroad as an upholsterer. He liked to drink beer, and he hated yard work. So he decided, probably after drinking some of the eight cases of beer he always had close at hand in the garage, to do away with his yard.

In 1968 he started little projects like embedding marbles in his wood fence. Pretty. Concrete, wood, and metal pieces started covering the yard, until the grass was gone completely. Wife Mary didn't object, possibly because she enjoyed dipping into those cases of beer in the garage along with John.

Trying to stave off the ever-present hot sun in Houston, John had the idea to put some empty beer cans to work. Beer can pieces cut and tied together, hanging from the eaves, provided shade and tinkled nicely in the wind. It was cute and saved some money on John's electrical bills by shading the house a bit.

But if a few cans hanging off the eaves could help, how about attaching a solid layer of aluminum cans to the walls of the house, like siding in 12 ounce sections? That's exactly what John started doing.

"I guess I just thought it was a good idea. And it's easier than painting," said John in one of the many interviews he gave about his house of cans. He seemed to love the attention. "It tickles me to watch people screech to a halt. They get embarrassed. Sometimes they drive around the block a couple of times. Later they come back with a car-load of friends."

His son Ronald told reporters his dad's favorite beer was "whatever's on special." After all, on a retirement fixed income, a man buying beer by a six-pack of cases must watch his pennies. Since neighbors helped drink John's beer, let's hope some of them bought a few cases for him as well.

Ripley's Believe It or Not came one time, and estimated there were more than 50,000 beer cans recycled in John's interesting way. While Ripley's and others considered John's hobby art, John didn't. "Some people say this is sculpture but I didn't go to no expensive school to get these crazy notions." That's one of the many great things about Texas: people can get crazy notions without paying tuition.

John's protestations during his life about his lack of artistic merit or attention fell on deaf artistic ears. After John's widow Mary moved out of the house in 2007, the Orange Show Center for Visionary Art took the house over and is in the process of restoration. After all, twenty plus years of Houston weather takes a toll on beer cans.

The Beer Can House is open for visitors on Saturdays and Sundays. Go to www.beercanhouse.org for details, and join their mailing list to keep up with the latest news and events around the Beer Can House.

## *Dissing Your Mercedes*

The AT&T Performing Arts Center, the last major venue in the Dallas arts district that hopes to jazz up business downtown, opened officially on October 19, 2009. A major social event, the opening for the Winspear Opera House meant 45,000 people coming to a series of events. But many got a surprise when they tried to park.

Modern Texans, at least modern rich Texans, treat their fancy cars like status symbols. So imagine how peeved some drivers of fancy cars became when they went to VIP parking and were turned away. That's right, turned away. Mercedes? Not good enough. Cadillac? Rolls Royce? Bentley? Ferrari? Nope.

"Make Way for Lexus Drivers" was the theme for the night. Drive a Lexus, get into VIP parking. As usual, money was the reason behind the strange behavior.

Naming rights for the opening festivities were bought by Lexus, hence the VIP parking situation. There are 850 parking spaces in the Center, but during the opening, only cars with a Lexus badge were treated like real VIPs.

Seizing on a good idea, or at least a way to make some extra bucks, the Dallas Symphony Orchestra did something similar when their season started in the fall of 2010. That time,

Audi bought the naming rights for the year. Audi cars were on display, and Audi drivers got free valet parking.

Think one or more of the symphony patrons will go buy an Audi so they can get better parking at the Symphony? Of course, but they may not admit that's what they did. But someone will, because showing off is as Texan as oil and money.

## *First Gold Country Record*

Would you believe Marion Slaughter, born in Jefferson on April 6, 1883, had the first gold country record? When he got to New York, he took the professional name Vernon Dalhart. He cribbed those names from the Texas towns, but nobody in New York, where he made his records, knew those names.

He moved his family (wife Sadie Le Moore-Livingston and son and daughter) to New York City in 1910. He worked in a piano warehouse (at least he was in the music business, as starving musicians everywhere would say) and took singing jobs when he could find them. Good singing jobs, too, such as Lt. Pinkerton in *Madame Butterfly* (that's the male lead) and in other operas and shows.

In 1916 he answered a newspaper ad and auditioned for Thomas Alva Edison, Mister "I invented the record player and you didn't" himself. Over the next seven years Dalhart made over 400 recordings of dance band vocals and light classical music under a series of pseudonyms. Because Dalhart / Slaughter used so many different names, as did most of the other recording artists of the day, it's hard to get exact number of recordings each artist made. Most agree Dalhart made more records in the 1920s than anyone else, but nobody can really prove it.

In 1924, the Victor Talking Machine Company was struggling. Whether Edison convinced Dalhart to go back to his roots and sing a couple of records in the hillbilly style, or (as we suspect) vice versa, that's what happened. Dalhart sang

"The Wreck of Old 97" with "The Prisoner's Song" on the flip side. The "Wreck of Old 97" was about a deadly train crash in Virginia when the speeding locomotive hit the curve in the 75-foot high Stillhouse Trestle going too fast, derailing and falling over the edge into Cherrystone Creek. Weren't the songs in the 20s cheerful?

Modern interjection: the popular alternative country band from Dallas named the Old 97's got their name from the song about the train wreck. And folks as famous as Johnny Cash covered the song, so tragedy sometimes powers music (see opera plots, especially by Verdi, for confirmation).

> *Yesterday is not ours to recover, but tomorrow is ours to win or lose.*
> — *Lyndon B. Johnson*

Dalhart essentially saved Victor, because his hillbilly songs sold over six million records, a huge number in the 1920s. In fact, no other non-holiday record sold that many copies in the first 70 years of the recording business.

By singing songs from his childhood in Texas (Jefferson until he was 10 years old, then Dallas until he moved to New York City), Dalhart made recording history. When he recorded "Home on the Range" in 1927, be became country music's first real star. Texas may not have the Grand Ol' Opry, but we can claim the first million-selling country artist.

## Carnegie Libraries
Andrew Carnegie sent over $600,000 to build 32 libraries in the state of Texas. The first, in Pittsburgh in 1898, received $5,000. Alas, it burned in 1939.

The last, in Mount Vernon, was in 1917. There wasn't enough money left in the Carnegie program to buy books, but locals chipped in and the place opened with 4,000 books two years later.

Cleverly, most Carnegie libraries in Texas were built to provide multiple functions, such as auditoriums. Renting those extra rooms out for events provided money to keep the libraries going.

Today, only five Carnegie library buildings in the state of Texas retain their original use. They are located in Ballinger, Bryan, Franklin, Jefferson and Stamford. The other library buildings have either been destroyed or have converted to other uses.

## The Bronte Club

The first literary book club in Texas was started in 1855 by schoolteacher Viola Shive (she remarried and became Viola Case in 1862). The Victoria Female Academy, started by Viola and first husband John R. Shive in 1848, was a missionary effort by the Shives to bring stern morality and intense learning to Texas, an area they considered educationally and spiritually destitute. And you thought complaining about Texans being educationally and spiritually destitute was a modern hobby.

Shive was an old school Presbyterian minister, and Texas was still the Wild West. To encourage the students to read, Viola started with a collection of 11 books kept under her bed. Once a week she would lend them to the students. Being a proper school, the girls would discuss books as part of their education, but the Bronte Club grew and outlasted the founding school, and the founder.

During the Civil War scholarship suffered as members focused on the war effort. But when the men-only Press Club of New York City gave a banquet for Charles Dickens in 1868 and pointedly excluded women, interest in women-only clubs soared around the country. This triggered a rebirth of the Bronte Club as well.

By 1873 the Club belonged more to the community than the school, and officially changed its name to the Bronte

Literary Club in 1880. Older girls and young married women expanded the ranks, and their group sent a delegate to the first meeting of the Texas Federation of Women's Clubs in Tyler in 1898. Then they dropped the Literary part again in 1901. Insert your own "women can be so dang fickle" joke here.

All manner of civic and philanthropic deeds were performed by the Bronte club during the 1900s, including bringing Eleanor Roosevelt to speak to an audience of 2,500 in December 1940. The Club ran the Bronte Library, the book-lending portion of their activities, until 1975, when they turned it over to the city and county and renamed it the Victoria Public Library.

Aren't you glad the women started this club? Can you imagine what type of books would have been in the first batch if they searched under the beds of the men and boys?

## *Closeup on J.R.*

Cue the scenery-chewing actors: it's time for *Dallas* the TV show. Starting in 1978 as a five-part miniseries, the show lasted 13 seasons to 1991. In the early days, all filming was done in the Dallas area, but toward the end of the run costs forced the production back to Hollywood. Including several reunion made-for-TV movies, there were 357 episodes produced.

Focus was initially supposed to be on Bobby Ewing, J.R.'s brother, and his new bride, Pam. However, J.R.'s oily scheming and dastardly deeds struck a chord with the viewing audience, and soon you could have renamed the series *The J.R. Show* and no one would have cared.

But people did care when that scheming weasel J.R. Ewing, deservedly in the minds of many, was gunned down in his office late at night as the cliffhanger at the end of Season Two. No TV show before or since created a buzz on the public side of the TV screen like *Dallas* did that summer. Spoiler Alert: J.R. survived.

The Southfork Ranch, fictional home of the Ewing family, has long been a conference and meeting center. As a point of pride, we point out that Larry Hagman, who created the character of J.R. Ewing and also Major Tony Nelson in the earlier sitcom *I Dream of Jeannie*, was born in Fort Worth.

## Book'em, Walker

Following *Dallas*, the TV show *Walker, Texas Ranger* took up filming in the Dallas and Fort Worth areas. After all, the production facilities and trained crew were still around, and few law enforcement agencies in the world have the cache of the Texas Rangers. The show ran for eight years (1993-2001) and 203 episodes, including a made-for-TV movie.

Martial arts expert Chuck Norris, star of many tough guy action movies in the 1970s and 80s, donned the star and a Stetson as a Texas Ranger on TV. While entertaining to many, whether as an action show or a campy hoot, *Walker, Texas Ranger* should not ever be confused as an example of realistic police work, and certainly not an honest depiction of the Texas Rangers.

As difficult as it is to perform a roundhouse kick to the head while wearing cowboy boots, Norris' character managed that feat at least twice every episode. Most kicks were replayed more often, and in slower motion, than winning touchdowns in the Super Bowl.

Bullets flew around that show almost as fast as Chuck Norris' feet. True to life? Not even close. During a talk to a group that included several Texas Hysterical Society members, retired Texas Ranger Bryan Clark (R.I.P.) was asked about the gunplay in *Walker, Texas Ranger*.

"If a Ranger pulled a gun, he'd have to do paperwork for six months," said Clark. "If he fired the gun, there was 18 months of paperwork waiting. And if a Ranger actually shot anyone, he'd reach retirement age before the paperwork was finished."

Among local Dallas actors, the joke was everyone met Chuck Norris by looking up his nose. No, Chuck isn't that tall, but locals were often cast as dead people, usually bad guys either killed or beaten up by Norris. From the bad guy's point of view, the camera would show Walker looking down at yet another vanquished foe. After the scene, Norris would help the actor up and introduce himself.

## Bluebonnets on the Byways

Lady Bird Johnson gets most of the credit for her work during the 50s and 60s, but the Texas Department of Transportation started planting wildflowers by highways in the 1920s. As Lyndon moved up the political ladder, Lady Bird encouraged planting more and more native plants and wildflowers that reminded her of the Texas Hill Country. The highway department now sows from 30,000 to 60,000 pounds of flower seeds along the highways to keep Texas drivers entertained. And looking at bluebonnets, the Texas State Flower, by the side of the road is much easier on your neck than leaf peeping.

## World's Largest Honky Tonk

Sure, *Urban Cowboy* was filmed in Houston at Gilley's, a pretty big bar when it was open, with over 44,000 square feet. But that's less than half the size of Billy Bob's in the Fort Worth Stockyards that includes over 127,000 square feet. That's nearly three acres inside, and over 20 acres outside for parking.

The building was originally built in 1910 as an open-air barn for use during the Fort Worth Stock Show. Prize cattle roamed where dancers now boot scoot. In 1936, as part of the Texas Centennial Project, a tower was added and the barn was enclosed. During World War II Globe Aircraft built airplanes for the war effort. Billy Bob's opened as the "World's Largest

Honky Tonk" on April 1, 1981 (no fooling).

6,028 people can be inside at one time (while making the Fire Marshal real nervous, and real upset if one more steps through the door) spread across multiple dance floors, stages, and bar areas. The world's record for most beer sold in one night belongs to Billy Bob's during a Hank Williams, Jr. concert: more than 16,000 bottles. Merle Haggard set another world record when he bought a round of drinks for the whole club. Buying the most drinks at once is probably not a record anyone else wants to challenge, so Merle may keep that record.

The place did great for a time, but by January 1988 some big projects that didn't work and loose management ran the joint into bankruptcy. But such a place is too important to let stay dead, and new investors cranked it back up by November the same year.

Many, many, *many* TV shows and movies have been filmed at Billy Bob's. Since the new owners took over, they've also created a record label named "Live at Billy Bob's." The Country Music Association awarded Billy Bob's Venue of the Year, the Academy of Country Music named it Country Music Club of the Year five times, and the Country Music Association named it Club of the Year twice.

## *Howdy from Big Tex*

If it's Big Tex, then it's the State Fair of Texas, held late September into October in Dallas at Fair Park. Of all the state fairs, this is the biggest and the best (of course).

Big things abound, such as Big Tex. After opening on the road as a giant Santa in Kerens for the Chamber of Commerce in 1949, Big Tex came to the State Fair and stayed (he got his AARP card in 2002, along with a huge cake). In 1963, Big Tex got a hinge in his jaw so he could talk to fairgoers as well as the media that cover his erection each year. You know, when they stand him up for everyone to see. It's a really big deal on local TV.

177

Something even bigger at the fair is the Texas Start Ferris wheel. At 212 feet, the Star is the largest Ferris wheel in North America. It arrived in 1985, just in time for the Texas Sesquicentennial (150th birthday).

Unfortunately, the fair didn't start out big. The Dallas State Fair and Exposition, a private company started in January 1886, got off to a rancorous start as disagreements led to a split that led to two fairs opening that year. One was at Fair Park, while the second was just north of town. Both built facilities, including racetracks, and both lost money as you would expect. The fair up north started one day before the one at Fair Park, guaranteeing neither would succeed. Cooler heads, and empty bank accounts, prevailed, and the two groups merged into the Texas State Fair and Dallas Exposition. Not competing with themselves allowed the single State Fair to become a bit more of a success.

> *You know you're in Texas when the weatherman says the cold front will drop the temperature down to about 90 degrees.*

Famous folks came to the Fair, which helped draw crowds. Notables included a concert by John Philip Sousa and appearances by William Jennings Bryan, Carrie Nation, and Booker T. Washington.

Some bad luck hit, with a grandstand collapsing during a fireworks show, and the main exhibit building burning down in 1902. But the worst luck was when the Texas Legislature banned gambling on horse races, which had been the Fair's largest revenue stream. To avoid ruin, the owners sold the land and buildings to the city of Dallas in 1904 with a deal that set aside a time for the State Fair each fall.

The change of management did wonders for the Fair, and over 300,000 people bought tickets in 1905. Still the only Fair in the US that includes an auto show, the one in Dallas started over 100 years ago in 1904 (big attractions: rubber tires and DVD players to keep the kids entertained). President William Howard Taft visited in 1909, and two years later Woodrow Wilson came to the Fair and gave a speech (and no doubt had a corny dog). Over one million visitors attended in 1916, but World War I activities canceled the Fair in 1918 as Fair Park was drafted into use as a military encampment.

The Music Hall was built in 1925 and provides a venue for traveling shows from Broadway and other concerts to this day (although it's no longer home to the Dallas Symphony Orchestra or the Dallas Opera). The Texas-Oklahoma football game started their annual run at the Cotton Bowl, on the other side of the Fair from the Music Hall, in 1929.

On October 11, 1956, a 20-year-old singer named Elvis Presley gave a concert to 2,000 screaming teenagers (1,948 of whom were girls) at the State Fair Main Stage. This crowd shattered the record for attendance at an outdoor concert in Texas.

About a million people per week (during the three week run) attended the State Fair during the 1990s, and the good times show no signs of slowing down now. Come to Dallas during the Fair, have a corny dog and try the winners of the fried "whatever it is this year" contest. Life will be better.

### Line Your Birdcage With the Cedar Snag

You could do so in Dallas in 1849, as James W. Latimer and William Wallace moved the Paris, Texas, *Times* newspaper to Dallas and renamed it the *Cedar Snag*. Quickly realizing that name ranked high on the stupidity scale for newspaper names, the duo renamed it the *Herald* in 1850. After merging with the *Daily Times* in 1879 and then the *Daily Herald* on January 2, 1888, the name became the *Dallas Times-Herald*.

As the *Dallas Time-Herald*, the paper kept going until December 9, 1991. After being gobbled by media conglomerate Belo Corporation, owners of the *Dallas Morning*

179

*News* (often referred to as the *Dallas Morning Snooze* because it was the more conservative and staid newspaper) shut down their competitor the *Times-Herald* and took over their subscribers.

The *Times-Herald* had more Sunday circulation than the *Morning Snooze* in 1977, and was named one of the top five newspapers in the South by *Newsweek* in 1975. Yet in another brilliant example of big business mismanagement, then owners Times Mirror Group sold the paper to a local group that cleverly led the paper to irrelevance and near bankruptcy. Of course, being the afternoon paper in a world moving to morning papers didn't help. The last straw? When the Belo Corporation bought exclusive rights to 26 Universal Press Syndicate features, keeping them out of the *Times-Herald*. People love their funnies, and losing them pushed the weak paper further down until selling out was the only option left. Sad.

But when you start your corporate life with the name the *Dallas Cedar Snag*, how can you overcome that burden? And what in the world does a cedar snag have to do with news? And what exactly is a cedar snag?

## Beauty and the Book

Women tend to buy more books than men, especially fiction, and they go to hair salons much more often than men. So when Kathy L. Patrick (Kat to her many, many friends) opened up a beauty salon on January 18, 2000, she combined her two passions into one store. Behold, Beauty and the Book, in Jefferson, out in the piney woods of East Texas.

The *Oxford American Magazine*, published at the time by famous lawyer turned author John Grisham, sent a writer and photographer to cover the opening. That initial publicity magnified as Kat Patrick, owner of the only hair salon slash bookstore in the entire civilized world (as far as we know) made for good quotes and better stories. And the hair fixin' ain't bad, either.

Kicking it up a notch, Kat started the Pulpwood Queens of East Texas book club. Signers and speakers at the hair/book club have included Kinky Friedman (born in Chicago, but a long-time Honorary Texan for his band Kinky Friedman and the Texas Jewboys, a play on Bob Wills and His Texas Playboys) during the time he was running for Governor of Our Great State. *Golden Girl* Rue McClanahan signed books there, as did Pat Conroy, Elizabeth Berg, and Rick Bragg. Tying the book and beauty theme together perfectly, supermodel (and *Sports Illustrated* Swimsuit model) and author Paulina Porizkova also came through. The Texas Hysterical Society Head Honcho will bestow Honorary Texan honors on Ms. Porizkova as soon as possible, but only in person.

Now there are over four hundred Pulpwood Queen Book Clubs around the U.S., and the Queens have gone international with members and clubs in ten foreign countries. For men, the clubs offer Timber Guy Book Club Selections. Kat Patrick gained even more notice with her book, *"The Pulpwood Queens' Tiara Wearing, Book Sharing Guide to Life"* in 2008. Check out the life philosophy that makes tiaras every day wear at www.PulpWoodQueen.com.

Books should be fun, and the Pulpwood Queens make sure they are. Over 500 authors have been involved with various events at Beauty and the Book or a Pulpwood Queens meeting. If you have a chance, take part in their annual Girlfriend Weekend Author Extravaganza that ends with the Great Big Ball of Hair Ball.

### Nuclear Polka

Where else but Texas could you find the world's best new wave polka band? Brave Combo burst onto the scene in 1979, playing polka heavily flavored with salsa, meringue, rock, klezmer, cumbia, conjunto, zydeco, cha cha, the blues, and classical music. No genre is safe when Brave Combo hits the stage.

How famous are they? They've won two Grammy Awards from their seven Grammy nominations. Their music is in movies and TV, including playing themselves in animation on *The Simpsons*. When David Byrne of Talking Heads got married, he hired Brave Combo to play his wedding reception.

From *The Simpsons* to some shows for PBS is a wide range. Check them out at www.brave.com/bo or www.bravecombo.net.

## *Wiccan Prisoner Complains*

Of course, this isn't really news, because all "guests of the state" complain about everything every day. Bad food, bad clothes, lousy bed, the fact that armed guards and iron bars stop them from going home each night, and that they can't decorate their cells with Samurai swords.

But let's hand it to Charles Arthur Roberts, a guest of the state in Edinburg, for finding something new to complain about: being discriminated against because he's a Wiccan. No, not the Marvel comic book hero William "Billy" Kaplan who can generate lightning and spells to make people do his bidding, but the neopagan religion and form of witchcraft updated to our modern age. The news story about Roberts doesn't say if he's a Gardnerian or Alexandrian Wicca adherent or if he follows the Minnesota Luther Wiccans and must bring a potluck dish to every church function.

Roberts filed a federal lawsuit against the Texas Department of Criminal Justice in general and the Chaplaincy Department in particular claiming they refuse to accommodate his religious practices. After all, the suit whines in legalese, the Chaplaincy Department helps the Protestant, Catholic, and Muslim prisoners, but is showing him no Wiccan love.

Since one tenet of Wicca, a nature-based religion with both a God and a Goddess, seems to be running around naked in the woods, such practice would seem to be in obvious conflict with being in prison. We doubt Wiccans would accept running around naked in the prison yard as an acceptable substitute, and we're sure the other prisoners might, ah, express displeasure at Roberts running about bare as a newborn baby while casting spells on them and spouting off about the Triple Goddess and Horned God. Just a thought, but that seems it might lead to general disorder and mayhem, and probably more lawsuits from Baptists annoyed by naked pagan rituals.

> *If Texas were a sane place, it wouldn't be nearly as much fun.*
> *— Molly Ivins, Honorary Texan*

Roberts claims to have made multiple requests for a Wiccan volunteer to help him hold proper services, but the state has yet to find someone. Perhaps the problem is the lack of Wiccan volunteers available for prison service in Edinburg. If that's the case, the local Wiccan community should step up. Or perhaps the prison officials can't stop laughing at his requests, which may be unprofessional but certainly understandable.

"I have been dealing with the defendants for a year to get things for my religion but they have not tried to get anything started, which is a violation of my Constitutional rights," said Roberts. He doesn't address the issue of being sentenced to five years in prison for an aggravated assault case, which doesn't seem very Wiccan. He also doesn't mention why he was denied parole in July 2007 and will be kept for the full term of his full sentence until December 2011, fairly unusual in today's crowded prison world.

When you get out, young Wiccan Charles Arthur Roberts, feel free to come back and act as a volunteer yourself for other incarcerated Wiccans. Do some good, and stop assaulting people in an aggravated manner and winding up in jail. Prison is not Wicca friendly, as you have learned.

## 101.1 FM

Smack in the middle of the Dallas FM radio band is where you'll find WRR, the classical radio station owned by the City of Dallas. The station was the first one west of the Mississippi and the first in Texas when it started broadcasting in 1920. By the summer of 1921 they received a provisional license and became official, unlike most other stations at the time. Of course, with only low-power signals and few listeners, radio wasn't a big business but more of a hobby for the gadget minded. Some may say it's not much of a business today, but they'd be wrong.

Starting out as a personal project of Henry Garrett, a Police and File Signal Supervisor for the City of Dallas, WRR's first broadcast "studio" was the Dallas Fire Department. As a way to send information to firefighters, the radio project of Supervisor Garrett was a success, more or less. But you know what happens when you leave an open microphone out: people think they are stars. Firefighters hanging around at the station between fires started telling jokes and playing music over the station.

The jokes must have been pretty good, because citizens started buying crystal radio sets to get in on the fun. This was, after all, a long time before TV, iPhones, and the Internet sucked up every free moment of the day.

> *Don't get your panties in a wad all the time. Just because you got insulted didn't mean someone was insensitive. Some people just like to be insulted. Don't be like that.*
> *— The Old Cowboy*

Moving downtown, the station started broadcasting from the fancy Adolphus Hotel in 1926. To pay for the nice digs, they started selling advertising in 1927. In the late 1930s, the station moved to its current location on the grounds of Fair

Park, the site of the Texas State Fair each October. FM broadcasts started in 1948 along with the AM band, but in 1978 the city sold the AM station, leaving just the FM station at 101.1 on your FM dial.

Still one of the rare radio stations owned by a city, WRR doesn't sound like a city-owned mess too often. However, the City Council meetings are broadcast over WRR every other Wednesday (unless the city is lucky enough for the politicians to be on vacation, where they can't create any more chaos or destruction). Otherwise, the city does a pretty good job of letting WRR play music and not politics.

While WRR seems to be doing well at this writing, City Council members get enticed every two or three years by an offer to sell the station or at least sell the frequency. So far, luckily, no council group has had enough short sighted members to gather a majority behind the notion of selling the station. Here's hoping the city politicians stay preoccupied and leave WRR alone. Well, they could give it a few more dollars now and then, but they should remember they make money each year from advertising, and still can ruin our Wednesdays every other week with city council meetings.

### *A Texas-Sized Church*

What do you do with a professional basketball arena when you build a new arena? In Dallas, you build American Airlines Center then tear down Reunion Arena. In Houston, when you retire the Compaq Center (you may remember it as The Summit), former home of the Houston Rockets, you turn the 16,800 seat arena into the biggest church (attendance wise) in the country. Welcome to Lakewood Church, an evangelical church headed by Joel Osteen and his wife and co-pastor, Victoria.

Old basketball arenas aren't cheap, and the Osteens paid a Texas sized sum of $11.8 million dollars, upfront in 2005, for the 30-year lease on the building. Then they spent another $75

185

million renovating the center and other church property. Then they made a deal with the Houston City Council to buy the place outright for $7.5 million more. That's a lot of bake sales.

Even with four services in English and one in Spanish each Sunday, the place is full and averages more than 43,500 attendees each week. They've come a long way since Joel's father John and mother Dodie started in 1959 in an abandoned feed store.

Father John started the TVangelical ministry early, and eventually reached over 100 countries via the airwaves. Joel and Victoria continue the TVanglical mission, including running KTBU-TV55, and independent television station in Houston.

## *Cowboy's Ten Commandments*

Posted way back when on the wall in the Cross Trails Church in Fairlie, Texas:

I.      Just one God
II.     Honor yer Ma & Pa
III.    No tellin' tales or gossipin'
IV.     Git yourself to Sunday meetin'
V.      Put nothin' before God
VI.     No foolin' around with another fellow's gal
VII.    No killin'
VIII.   Watch yer mouth
IX.     Don't take what ain't yers
X.      Don't be hankerin' for yer buddy's stuff

Y'all git that?

## *Texans and Chainsaws*

Believe it or not, the story used as the basis for the cult hit movie *Texas Chainsaw Massacre* didn't happen in Texas but in… Wisconsin. Yes, in barbarous murdering, Wisconsin wins this round against Texas.

Tobe Hooper (Texan), the writer and director of the movie called TCM by fans, visited relatives in Wisconsin as a youngster. During that time, a privacy-seeking farmer named Ed Gein hit the news big, as stories of his masks made from the skin of his victims became the seed that later sprouted into Leatherface. Gein needed a bunch more privacy, because he was ultimately convicted of necrophilia, cannibalism, and, obviously, murder. After all, you can't be convicted of necrophilia without a dead body.

And in Hooper's defense, who would go see a movie called *Wisconsin Chainsaw Massacre*? Wouldn't that have to be *Wisconsin Snow Shovel Murder*?

# Education

## *A Word to the Unwise*

If you use this book as a textbook for Texas history, you will laugh more than at any other textbook, but you will not pass the official state tests. The choice is yours, although you can split the difference and read your proper textbooks at school and this book for fun.

## *First College Arguments*

Want to see academicians get into a ruckus? Ask which Texas college or university was first, and stand back.

Those from Southwestern University in Georgetown (a bit north of Austin) claim they were first, but we need some asterisks by that entry. Southwestern proper wasn't official until 1872. But Southwestern fans point to Rutersville College, near La Grange, that was started in 1840. Combining Rutersville, Wesleyan College (1844), McKenzie College (1848) and Soule University (1856) in 1872 turned all four into Southwestern.

But fans of Austin College in Sherman (north of Dallas) claim to be the oldest college still operating under the original charter. The school was incorporated in November 1849 and modeled on the charter and ideals of Harvard, Yale, and Princeton. The school opened for students in the fall of 1850.

Fans of UT and Texas A&M will start spouting off about being started in 1839, when the Congress of the Republic of Texas set aside land for two universities. What the T-sippers and Aggies forget is that their doors didn't open for students until November 1882 and October 1876 respectively.

Baylor Baptists will then pipe up and talk about being organized in 1841. By the sin of omission they conveniently forget to mention they weren't chartered until 1845 and opened in 1846. Shame on those Baptists, but it does make for fun arguments.

Of course, most discussions in Texas about first revolve

around football teams. At the end of the season, there are no doubts, because of the excellent college football playoff system. Oops, wait, the "playoff system" is designed so six different schools can claim to be Number One. Guess we can't blame the academicians for not being able to answer the "who's first" question when football fans can't answer who's Number One either.

> It's important for us to explain to our nation that life is important. It's not only life of babies, but it's life of children living in, you know, the dark dungeons of the Internet.
> – George W. Bush, Honorary Texan

## University of Texas at Austin

The lead campus in the University of Texas System that includes 15 campuses, UT was built on land set aside by the Congress of the Republic of Texas in 1839, as was Texas A&M. Before that, in 1827, the Constitution for the Mexican state of Coahuila y Tejas mentioned a public university in what was to become Texas. Do we owe UT to the largesse of the Mexican government? Not really, but that's an interesting thought, and the Mexican government had that thought first.

A land-based endowment called the Permanent University Fund received fifty leagues of land (231,400 acres) in 1839, then a million acres granted by the Constitution of 1876 (mandating a "university of the first class," and another two million acres from the Legislature in 1883. Grazing rights from the donated land were to help fund UT and Texas A&M.

Minor details after 1839 like joining the Union, the Mexican American War, the Civil War, and Reconstruction delayed the start of UT until November 17, 1882, when the cornerstone was laid for the first Main Building. Ashbel Smith, elected first president of the Board of Regents a year earlier, said, "Smite the rocks with the rod of knowledge, and fountains of unstinted wealth will gush forth." Even then, politicians were blowhards. School started officially on September 15, 1883, and was held in temporary space in the Capitol until part of the main building was finished in January 1884. Wow, UT started out in portable buildings, somewhat like the ones you see beside just about every public school today.

College Hill in Austin was the original site of the forty-acre tract for the campus, close to the Capital building. True to form, the first addition to the campus, in 1897, was an athletic field. The original area, sometimes called the Forty Acres, was henceforth known as the Forty Acres and Football. Some consider football as the main reason for UT even today (at least during winning seasons).

> *Rarely is the question asked, is our children learning?*
> *– George W. Bush, Honorary Texan*

Perhaps Ashbel Smith and his "fountains of unstinted wealth" meant something more prosaic: oil was found on the UT campus in 1923. How much more Texan could you get than finding oil on the campus of the state university? Much of that income was put to work building fireproof buildings in place of the temporary frame structures built to hold the growing student population, especially after World War I. Ma Ferguson, The Guv at the time, said about the need for new buildings, "To the average man who sees the miserable looking buildings at the University, it would appear the state is making an effort to store up hay instead of to store up knowledge."

The end of World War II and the GI Bill brought another flood of students, and therefore more temporary frame buildings. Had to have somewhere to educate the 15,118 students enrolled in 1946-7, but the building funds caught up and replaced the frame buildings with nice permanent ones soon after.

Now UT has the fifth largest enrollment in the United

States, but was the largest school during the years 1997-2003. Over 50,000 students (undergrad and graduate students) along with 16,500 faculty and staff strive mightily each and every day to "smite the rocks with the rod of knowledge." And win football games. And party.

## The Killer Daisies

No, not an environmental horror film. Killer Daisies is the official mascot of the Hockaday School (www.hockaday.org), "an independent college preparatory day and boarding school for girls, Prekindergarten through 12th Grade." Lest you think "Killer Daisies" sounds like a mix of punk and hippy dippy, Hockaday is about as far away from punk and hippy dippy as you can get. This school with a huge campus in one of the most expensive residential areas of North Dallas exists to prepare young women of means to rule the world.

And "means" is important, since the cream of the female upper crust in Dallas (upper crust males go to St. Marks) pays around $17,650 for grade school to attend (2010 tuition). High school? $23,076, unless you're an international student who lives on campus. Then the tag is $45,760 per year. And Hockaday says they provide $3 million in financial aid spread across their 1,100 or so students.

Being rich gets you an outstanding education. Average class size is 15. Compare that to an average suburban school class size of 32 to 35. Educational professionals will tell you 15 students per class is the perfect number to maximize learning. Hmm, isn't it lucky how Hockaday managed to have the exact perfect number for their average class size?

The results are what you might expect when taking the top girls from successful families and giving them the best education. Half the students taking AP (Advanced Placement) tests in 2010 scored a 5, the top rating. Three quarters received either a 4 or 5. Many suburban high schools don't have but a handful of AP test scores of 5 per year.

193

Hockaday is named for Ela Hockaday, the first teacher. Born in Ladonia, Texas, in 1875, Ms. Hockaday and fellow teacher and "special friend" Sarah Trent tired of the teaching racket and bought a farm in Falfurrias in 1912. A bad summer, and the realization that teaching is far easier than plowing, made Miss Hockaday quite receptive when some well-to-do parents came looking for experienced teachers to start a new school. Miss Hockaday and Miss Trent quickly traded in their seeds for schoolbooks and started Miss Hockaday's School for Girls in 1913.

> *The Texas Board of Education demanded that public schools for girls spend two days a week on needlework (1871).*

Hockaday has more National Merit Finalists than any other girls' school in the U.S. One hundred percent of all graduating seniors are accepted to "prestigious colleges and universities" which is not a surprise. If your parents can pay $16,355 to send you to half-day prekindergarten classes, you will almost certainly get into a good college.

Upper crust jokes notwithstanding, Hockaday takes outstanding young women and makes them better. A senior class of around 300 girls in 2010 included 16 National Merit Finalists and 16 National Merit Semifinalists. That's more than most school districts, much less relatively small high schools.

### The Lions

The St. Marks School of Texas (www.smtexas.org) is a non-sectarian private school for grades 1-12 that grew out of the tradition of the Episcopal Church. Officially separate from Hockaday, the St. Marks Lions functions as the brother school to the Hockaday Killer Daisies, and students from each school attend special classes at the other.

Developing a bit later than their sister school (but boys always develop later than girls), St. Marks developed by merging three private schools: The Terrill School (1906-1944), which became the foundation of the Cathedral School (1944-1950), and the Texas Country Day School (1933-1950). Merging the Texas Country Day School with the Cathedral School made the non-sectarian pitch a little harder to say with a straight face, especially since the merged school mandated Episcopalian Chapel services.

Since the Terrill School officially opened in 1906, before Hockaday, St. Marks' boys argue with their Hockaday girlfriends about who came first. The Hockaday girls agree the boys did, but that it doesn't matter (but privately, they say it does). The real foundation of St. Marks was the Texas Country Day School, which opened in 1933. The current name of "St. Marks School of Texas" appeared in 1953, making the boys even further behind the girls in many ways.

The idea behind the Texas Country Day School was to provide "a school in the country for city boys in the tradition of the English prep schools." In 1933 Preston Road and Walnut Hill Lane was in the country, but today that area has more mansions full of corporate bigwigs than any area in Dallas besides the towns of Highland Park and University Park (both surrounded by Dallas but officially separate, and UP is the home of SMU).

> *I have opinions of my own – strong opinions – but I don't always agree with them.*
> *– George H. W. Bush, Honorary Texan*

Tuition starts a bit higher than at Hockaday ($19,200 for 2010-2011) but ends up about the same ($23,766 for seniors). The school offers about $2.1 million in scholarships and aid, and a payment plan. But the price does include lunch each day. Bet the St. Marks boys don't get "mystery meat" like the public school kids get.

Buildings on the 40-acre campus are usually named after the principal benefactor, which is why the school's math and science quadrangle is named after the founders of Texas Instruments. The Lamar Hunt family (founder of the Dallas Texans football team which moved to become the Kansas City Chiefs of the NFL) donated a new football stadium.

Smaller than Hockaday, St. Marks has around 830 students. Like Hockaday, class sizes in middle and high school are around 15 students. Of the 2009 class, 30 were National Merit Semi-Finalists. The median SAT score, out of a maximum 2400, was 2130. The most recent 87 graduates had no trouble getting into their choice of 44 highly rated colleges and universities. Honorably, six of those 87 went to military academies.

Alumni include H. Ross Perot, Jr., Steve Miller, Boz Scaggs, Tommy Lee Jones (Academy Award winner), and the Wilson brothers, Luke and Owen. While Luke graduated in 1990, Owen was supposedly expelled before graduating. Since no one in Hollywood returns our calls, we couldn't get Owen on the record about his school shenanigans.

Of course, an amazing number of corporate executives and big-dog lawyers in Texas graduated from St. Marks. It's always easier to make a multimillion-dollar deal when you can "motivate" your opponent with blackmail material from the 7th grade.

Robert K. Hoffman, Class of 1965, went on to Harvard (that's not unusual for St. Marks graduates). He was an editor for the *Harvard Lampoon*, the school's famous comedy slash satire magazine (that is unusual). He and three other editors then founded *National Lampoon* in 1970, the comedy slash satire magazine that begat wackiness such as movies, the most famous of which is *Animal House*. That's wonderful. Thanks, Robert. He sold his *National Lampoon* shares in 1975 to buy a modern painting that became the first piece in a collection that grew to 224 pieces worth over $150 million. That's wacky. He died in Dallas in August of 2006, which is sad.

## Houston's Kinkaid School Starts and Stays Coed

While the Dallas' high-end private schools, Hockaday and St. Marks, keep the boys and girls separated except for a few classes between campuses and social events, the Kinkaid School in Houston claims to be the oldest independent coeducational school in Houston. Since the first school to educate boys and girls in the same class was Baylor University in 1865, Kinkaid's start in 1906 shows it got into the coed business rather early.

Started by Margaret Hunter Kinkaid in 1904 in the dining room of her house, the student body consisted of five students. The driving force behind the opening of her own school? She got married, and the policy of the Houston School District at the time said married female teachers were not welcome. As a Texan with linage directly back to the Old Three Hundred group of settlers brought in by Stephen F. Austin to help settle Texas, the new Mrs. Kinkaid had a keen sense of independence and justice.

Officially the school started in 1906, after a break for Kinkaid to have her second son. She always referred to the 1906 date as the real opening of the school. By the 1920s the house was overflowing with students, and Kinkaid got serious about the business of education and the need for a real school. Somehow she convinced many of the biggest wigs in the Houston business community to be on her new Board of Trustees, and they helped her open the first non-homestead school building. They kept growing and growing, and now have a 40 acre campus in Piney Point Village, an enclave of Houston.

Tuition in 1906 was $90. Tuition in 2010-2011 was $13,940 for prekindergarten up to $18,800 for high school. On the plus side, the extra money does provide Internet access, which wasn't the case in 1906.

Nearly 1,300 students are Kinkaid Falcons today. And unlike St. Marks and Hockaday, the school is coed and has been since the first group gathered around Margaret Kinkaid's dining room table in 1904.

> *The politically correct folks are getting a little too PC for their own good, at least in Texas. One elementary school demands the children play Cattle Management Specialists and Native Americans during recess.*

## *Grab Your Ankles*

It might seem odd that a state the executes more prisoners than any other state in the union, and in fact more than most other states combined, would ban corporal punishment in schools. Not wanting to seem odd, or at least not odd about this, Texas maintains corporal punishment. In fact, one of four school paddlings nationally happens in Texas.

Some school districts banned the paddle, but not all. And some that banned the practice reconsidered, such as the good people in central Texas (often called the HOT area for Heart of Texas, and a description of summer) and the Temple school district. The school board voted unanimously in the spring of 2010 to pick up the paddle after putting it down for a time. The city's 14 schools, including one high school, decided the paddle was the type of "incentive" students needed to keep their focus on school and not shenanigans.

Student behavior at the one high school improved greatly, according to administration. This in spite of the fact only one student got paddled. However, if the Temple school officials lied about the discipline improvements, should we paddle them?

> *You can't fix stupid.*
> *– Ron White, comedian*
> *Good advice on why many Texans refuse to argue with Yankees. Also, a wonderful standup comedy routine from native son Ron White (available on DVD).*

## Lawyers at "Work"

It's hard to tell whether this is a story of just desserts or just crazy, but the University of Texas (UT in Austin) sent a legal notice to Apple Computer about an iPhone application in the Apple App Store. Since Apple likes to sue people right and left if they happen to use a lower case "i" in some name, and lately even if people use the word "pad" in something, the legal department at Apple should be used to this. Well, maybe they're just used to sending threatening letters, but not receiving.

The letter threatened, politely but firmly, Apple for selling an application for their iPhone named iTexas. It sounds like a handy little app, since it helps students by listing information such as menus from the cafeterias on campus, shows campus maps, and even tallies Bevo Bucks, the private money accounts for students.

Why is UT upset? Because they have an app that does the same thing? Nope. Their app lists all sorts of press crap and sports information, totally useless to the vast majority of students.

UT is upset because the app uses the word "Texas" in the name, and UT claims Texas is their trademark. You read that right – UT claims the trademark to the word Texas in all its glory.

> *The difference between genius and stupidity is that genius has its limits.*
> *– The Old Cowboy*

We can accept that the school controls certain names, like Bevo, the football team mascot, and Lady Longhorns for their girls' basketball team, but Texas? Really? Huh? Really? UT claims to control the name Texas? Wasn't the state here before UT? Do no lawyers at UT understand the concept of prior art in trademark and patent cases? Does no one at UT have a clue how stupid this looks?

Officially, the Texas Hysterical Society proclaims this Above and Beyond Stupid. Hey, crazy UT lawyers, want a piece of us? Fill out your nasty legal forms and lawsuits and send them to:

John Doe
Texas Hysterical Society
123 Main Street
Anywhere, USA 12345

## *Aggies Awake*

Texas A&M University, located in College Station, kind of started in 1839 when the Fourth Congress of the Republic of Texas donated about 231,400 acres (officially fifty leagues, whatever a league is) for the endowment of two universities or colleges. This early date is why A&M folks say they are the first public university in Texas, although UT was part of the same endowment. In 1856 the State of Texas authorized selling some land to create the Permanent University Fund, but nothing was built before the Civil War.

In 1862, the federal government kept the university ball rolling by passing the Morrill Act auctioning public lands to establish endowments for schools of higher education (didn't Texas do that already?). The only catch was the at least one college must be a place "where the leading object shall be, without excluding other scientific and classical studies and including military tactics, to teach such branches of learning as are related to agriculture and the mechanical arts." Hence the A&M in Texas A&M.

Because of the 1839 original act by the Republic of Texas, Aggies claim to be the oldest school in Texas, although they claim lots of things. Anything started during the Republic of Texas does get bragging rights, however. The nickname Aggies came from the Agriculture and Mechanical part of the name. Female students are often referred to as Maggies.

| *Lagoon: French Aggie.* |
| --- |

Despite the 1839 date claimed by the Aggies, the first classes started on October 4th, 1876, at the Agricultural and Mechanical College of Texas, known to the in-crowd as Texas A.M.C. Six faculty members led the 40 students through their lessons. In accordance with the times, all students were white males. Out of accordance with the times, all students were required to participate in the Corps of Cadets and be schooled in all arts military.

After The University (as the UT people like to call it) started in Austin in 1883, A&M's student population dropped from a high of 258 students down to 108. Folks wondered why a state the size and population of Texas needed two entire universities, and wanted Texas A.M.C (Texas A&M) closed in favor of UT. Many UT fanatics still raise that issue today.

To the rescue came former Governor of Texas, and revered Confederate Brigadier General, Lawrence Sullivan Ross. Although born in Iowa Territory in 1838 as the fourth child of Catherine (Fulkerson) and Shapley Prince Ross (wow, what a name for a patriarch), General Ross came to Texas in 1839 because he wanted to close to his family as they moved to Texas. Since he was in Texas when Texas became a State, the Texas Hysterical Society declares him an Honorary Texan. The school elected him president in 1891.

Because parents wanted their sons to "be like Ross,"

enrollment jumped. Ross also started classes in the agricultural arts, as the stated charter demanded, rather than focusing on the early curriculum of classical studies, languages, literature, and applied mathematics. By the time General Lawrence Sullivan "Sul" Ross died suddenly on 1898, the school was on solid footing and well established. Sul Ross State University, in Alpine, was named in his honor.

Thanks to General Ross and the military expertise he brought to the school, Texas A&M regularly sends more graduates to the US Armed Forces than the service academies. He also started many Aggie traditions, such as the Aggie Ring, that live today.

## *Aggie Steam Tunnels*

One of the Aggie traditions today (but we can't blame this one on General Ross), is the search for the secret underground tunnels at the school. Rumor has it all sorts of fun things can be found in the tunnels originally built to carry steam between buildings in the winter.

The steam tunnels are still there, although the steam pipes are losing the battle against data and phone wires running between buildings. What can't be found in the tunnels are secret armories, secret club meeting sites, and ghosts. OK, maybe a ghost or two.

Officially, there are no artillery pieces from World War I hiding in the steam tunnel storage rooms, waiting to be loaded and fired by Doughboys in battle with the Kaiser. Absolutely not, so stop looking. There is, however, a firing range used by the Corps of Cadets. Unfortunately for conspiracy theorists, they use .22 rifles, not cannons.

While two secret societies, the True Texans and the Stikas, did exist on campus, they officially disbanded in the early 1950s. In fact, the True Texans announced their dissolution in the school newspaper. If there's anything you can trust in this world, it's the word of secret societies when given to student journalists.

In 1965, the night meat laboratory (wouldn't that be a great name for a heavy metal band?) manager had an accident with an electric saw, and bled to death before anyone knew there was a problem. Today, students swear there is a ghost in the tunnels and basements. According to reports, he endlessly wanders the halls, dragging one leg, and yelling "call 9-1-1" in an ethereally adamant voice.

If you go wandering in the steam tunnels, be careful. The pipes really do carry steam. The ticket for trespassing carries a fine and 200 hours of community service.

### Aggie Joke Samples

Out of the millions to choose from, here are six examples.

Why do Aggies hate M&Ms? They're too hard to peel.

How do you know an Aggie invented the toothbrush? Anyone else would have called it a teethbrush.

Did you hear about the Maggie (female Aggie) who had an abortion? She wasn't sure it was hers.

What do you call an Aggie's skeleton in a closet? The winner of a Hide and Go Seek contest.

An Aggie, a Longhorn (UT) and a Red Raider (Texas Tech) had been up to a little summertime mischief one night when the police came to the scene. All three quickly ran into the woods to escape, and each climbed a tree to hide in the leaves.

A police officer come to tree hiding the Longhorn, and yelled, "Is anybody up there?" The Longhorn said, "Meow, meow."

The officer went to the next tree, the one hiding the Red

Raider. "Is anybody up there?" the officer yelled. The Red Raider said, "Hoo, hoo, hooooo."

At the third tree, the one hiding the Aggie, the officer tried again. "Is anybody up there?"

The Aggie answered, "Moo, moo, mooooo."

An Aggie was out hunting, and walked into a little glade. There, on a blanket, a beautiful brunette lay sunbathing. Nude sunbathing. The Aggie walked closer, and yelled out, "Are you game?"

The brunette looked up, smiled, and beckoned the Aggie closer. "I sure am, big boy, I sure am."

So the Aggie shot her.

A plane at 30,000 feet trailing long white streaks is an Aggie cropduster.

An Aggie applied to be a police detective. The chief liked Aggies because they worked hard and never gave him trouble, but most couldn't pass the written test. To help this applicant, the chief tested him during the interview.

"Who killed Abraham Lincoln?" asked the chief.

"I don't know," answered the Aggie.

"Go home and think about it," said the chief.

When the Aggie got home, his wife asked if he got the job. "I think so. He already has me working on a case."

There are three types of Aggies: those who can count, and those who can't (count the number of jokes in this section).

## *Big Hole On Campus*

The University of Texas El Paso (known as UTEP) was once called the Texas State School of Mines and Metallurgy. Don't believe us? Go visit the mineshaft on campus.

Go rent the movie *Glory Road* and see the somewhat

fictionalized story of basketball coach Don Haskins. When UTEP appeared in the 1966 NCAA Men's Basketball Championship, they were the first ever to have an all-black starting lineup. UTEP shattered the unofficial color barrier for college basketball.

### Baylor vs. Huckins vs. Tyron

Just as UT fanatics like to call their school The University, Baylor acolytes often refer to their school as Thee University. Since the school was founded by the education society of the Texas Union Baptist Association in 1841, it dates back to the Republic of Texas days, and they regularly claim old school bragging rights, even though the school didn't actually open until 1846.

Three men, Robert E. B. Baylor, James Huckins, and William Milton Tyron, pushed this issue. R. E. B. Baylor won the rock-paper-scissors contest and was given the honor of putting his name on the school, which is kind of a shame because Huckins University has a nice ring to it. When asked where they studied, students could smile and say, "Huck U!"

### How Normal is Your College?

In 1903, Southwest Texas Normal School opened in San Marcos (between Austin and San Antonio, but closer to Austin). Designed to be a college for teachers, the "Normal" didn't mean the normal normal, but referred to the "norms" and guidelines for teaching. Then they tried the name Southwest Texas State Normal College in 1918, and Southwest Texas State Teachers College in 1923. They must have spent a fortune repainting signs and redoing stationary during those years.

After a quiet period, the Texas Legislature changed the name in 1959 to Southwest Texas State College, then in 1969 to Southwest Texas State University. In 2003, the name changed again to Texas State University – San Marcos.

Whatever the name, the school is the only major university in Texas to include a U. S. President in their alumni list: Lyndon Baines Johnson graduated from there in 1930.

Around 30,000 students attend Texas State University now, and the main campus has 225 building on 457 acres. Built on two hills favored by Indians in the days before Texas, the school has found a way to break the laws of physics. Everywhere you walk on campus is uphill. From a dorm on the quad to the library: uphill. From the library back to the dorm: uphill. The first person to figure out how this works deserves a Nobel Prize.

## *The Higher Education Hardware Store*

While much knowledge has been transferred between the shelves of all good hardware stores, not many such stores can make the claim they started a university. But on September 16, 1890, on the second floor of the B. J. Wilson Hardware store on the square in Denton, the first classes were held for the school that eventually became the University of North Texas.

They jumped the gun a bit, because the school's charter wasn't granted until June the next year. This could be the only example ever of a project that started in a hardware store actually finishing early.

The Texas Normal College and Teacher's Training Institute persevered, and by 1893 the school had earned the authority to confer state teaching certificates. Unfortunately, the paperwork from the state accidentally renamed the school the North Texas Normal College. Not slowing down for the name change, NTNC grew and grew and became the largest teacher training school in the southwestern U.S. by 1923. To celebrate their success, they renamed the place North Texas State Teachers College at Denton.

After World War II, as students flooded in, new disciplines beyond teacher certification became more and more important.

To illustrate the new approach, the school changed names again, this time dropping the "Teachers" part to become North Texas State College in 1949.

Continued growth in the number of students and disciplines offered, and the growing celebrity of the School of Music, prompted another change of name. In 1961, right before the fall semester, the place became North Texas State University.

> *A conclusion is too often the place where you got tired of thinking.*
>
> *— The Old Cowboy*

To reflect the fact the school was recognized as an emerging national research university (so said the Governor's Select Committee on Higher Education in 1986), something had to change. After much deliberation (building tension) the Powers That Be decided to – wait for it – change the name (anticlimax). The University of North Texas became the seventh name for the place in 1988.

> *Texas has yet to learn submission to any oppression, come from what source it may.*
>
> *— Sam Houston, #1 Honorary Texan*

The school mascot was chosen in 1922, and happily remained the Eagle for 80 years. However, in the spring of 2002, the Albino Squirrel Preservation Society began a noisy campaign to either replace the eagle mascot or add the albino squirrel as a secondary mascot. No joy. To add insult to the rejection injury, the albino squirrel that started all the mascot unrest was swooped up by a hawk. Grades went down immediately, because any student who saw the albino squirrel before a test parlayed that good luck omen into better grades. No squirrel meant a shorter Dean's List. It also appears being an albino squirrel is detrimental to hiding from predators.

As poorly as UNT's football team usually does, changing the mascot from the rather toothless eagle (really, eagles have no teeth) to the Albino Squirrels couldn't hurt. At least the UNT Albino Squirrels would have teeth and could bite you, then run away really fast and zoom up a tree. To determine whether they could do that while carrying a football requires further study. The Texas Hysterical Society is applying for a federal grant in order to better research this matter.

## *William Marsh Rice University*

Officially, Rice University in Houston is William Marsh Rice University. How all this came to be is a Texas type tale, even if much of it happened in New York City.

Born in Springfield, Massachusetts, in 1816, William Marsh Rice can't be blamed for not being Texan because there was no Texas at that time. He got here quickly. After starting to work in a general store at age 15, young William made it to Houston, Texas, after the Panic of 1837. He started supplying liquor to the Milam Hotel then received a headright certificate (legal grant of land to settlers) to 320 acres of Houston land (a big grant since most topped out at 100 acres. Perhaps young William plied an authority or two with some bottled potables?). By 1840 he had a first-class license for a mercantile business from the city. All that time and distance later, he was back in the general store business.

After a few partners and some expansion, William Rice and Company became a thriving export and import business that supplied plantations and settlers. Goods went through Rice and Company to and from New Orleans and New York for the most part. He also had a brig named the *William M. Rice* (seems he was proud of his name) that brought ice from the Boston area to Galveston each summer. Add the Capitol Hotel, Capitol Hotel Annex Building, and Houston Cotton Compress Company to his list, as well as being president of the Houston

Brick Works Company. Some records indicated Rice was the second richest man in Texas in 1860.

During the War of Northern Aggression he skipped down to Matamoros in Mexico, but left his home to be used as a military hospital. A bit conflicted, he owned 15 slaves, but the Union cause resonated with him. After the war he moved to New Jersey, but represented the Houston and Texas Central Railroad. He also retained the Capitol Hotel, which became the Rice Hotel.

In 1891 Rice incorporated and endowed the William Marsh Rice Institute "for the advancement of literature, science, and art." Even though living in the New York area, Rice's heart was still in Texas. He set aside half his wealth (about $4 million at the time) for the Rice Institute and the rest for his wife and other family. After his wife died in 1896 he redrew the will, adding more relatives. But the school endowment was still promised half his fortune.

> *You teach a child to read, and he or her will be able to pass a literacy test.*
> *– George W. Bush, Honorary Texan*

Now things get interesting. His valet and his lawyer thought they could get away with a little will rewriting and line their pockets. After all, they would only be bilking some distant relatives and a school that didn't exist.

After editing the will, the two got impatient that Rice didn't die according to their script. So they added some special effects to help him along. They killed him by suffocation (some accounts say poisoned with chloroform) on September 23, 1900.

Rice was pretty old when he died, so no one got excited about the death, until the co-conspirators made a mistake. The valet forged a huge check to the lawyer the next morning. The bank clerk noticed the check's payee was the lawyer, which may not be unusual, but that the name was misspelled. When the clerk tried to call Mr. Rice, the jig for the valet and lawyer was officially up.

Well, when rich people are involved, nothing moves fast. Investigation showed the lawyer had forged a variety of documents, including changes to the will. Lawyers complicated the trials and the distribution of assets, as they always do. The New York press had a field day, and the new century got a crime of the century right away.

After several years of wrangling, the valet and the lawyer went to jail, and the soon-to-be school got the money Rice set aside, finally, in 1904. Trustees had to interpret Rice's rather vague endowment instructions since there was nothing concrete about the endowed school. So they did something smart (not always the case with trustees) and hired a well-educated young man named Dr. Edgar Odell Lovett. How do we know Lovett was well educated? He had dual doctorates, one from the University of Virginia and one from the University of Leipzig.

Lovett went on a tour of the most advanced universities around the world. The goal was to spare no expense to build a great school. On September 23, 1912, the anniversary of Rice's murder, 77 students and a dozen faculty members opened the William Marsh Rice Institute.

> *Controversy, like beauty, is frequently in the eye of the beholder.*
>
> *– Lyndon Baines Johnson*

Thanks to the huge endowment ($4.6 million in 1900 equaled about $112 million in 2010), Rice opened with free tuition for the male and female students attending. In fact, the money pile was so big, students attended tuition free through 1963.

William Marsh Rice's instructions, and the trustees of the

school endowment, both aimed to establish a university "of the highest grade" that kept "the standards up and the numbers down." They have done so, because Rice is recognized for the quality of their students entering and the high level of instruction they receive. Rice University attracts smart kids who attract great job offers when they graduate.

In 2009, there were 3,279 undergraduate students. Since there are some public high schools in Texas with that many students, the numbers are certainly being kept "down" as per instructions.

There were also 2,277 graduate students (numbers kept down yet again, although that high ratio of graduates to undergraduates speaks to the highly technical disciplines offered that require advanced degrees). But since there are only five undergraduates for each faculty member, and 72 percent of the students accepted were in the Top 5 percent of their high school graduation classes, the "standards up" instruction has been followed as well.

High standards and low numbers have kept Rice at the top of Texas universities. Many count Rice as one of the "hidden ivies," as in Ivy League quality school. All this because William Marsh Rice, who started out as a grocery store clerk in Massachusetts, loved Texas and Texans.

### Texas School Book Tussles: Sound and Fury and No Books

Every 10 years, the Texas Board of Education revises school textbooks for one subject or another. The member of said Board are elected, and various political and religious groups often storm the ballot box and elect candidates with pointed agendas they hope to pack into school textbooks. How do they get away with this? Voters never expect some folks will pervert the education of Texas children to push their own views.

This concerns the people of the rest of the country because Texas is such a huge textbook market that publishers foist the Texas revisions on much of the rest of the country. California dictates schoolbooks through middle school, but leaves the choice of high school textbooks to individual districts. That means that although Texas has fewer total students, the high school market controlled by the state is so huge even California schools get sold the Texas book revisions. Boy, does that aggravate some of the progressive Californians.

Texas voters should know better by now. Here's a quote from Texas Governor O. B. Colquitt in 1911: "I had rather resign the Governor's office of Texas than to have my children studying a textbook in the public schools of Texas with Lincoln's picture left out of it, and I am the son of a Confederate soldier."

The battle got pretty fierce in 2009-2010 during the social studies sweep of updates. Revisions this time were on U.S. History since 1877. Fifteen State School Board members, elected every four years, manage the textbook changes. Since they are elected, there is no qualification for subject matter expertise. The result? The most powerful voice on the board in 2010, a dentist, took great delight in rewriting the history Texas students will learn.

> *You're never too old to learn something stupid.*
> *– The Old Cowboy*

A group of strongly conservative and religious members earned the nickname "the Block of Seven" because they voted as a block to block every liberal or secular suggestion made. Block O' Seven also introduced far right ideology whenever possible through means obvious and devious. For instance, they didn't want to make the election of President Obama an important day in history (first black President) but did want to list his full name, Barack Hussein Obama, which is a tactic used by those claiming Obama is not a U.S. Citizen (even though his birth certificate has been produced multiple times) with every single listing.

In another example, Thomas Jefferson was downplayed in discussions about the Era of Enlightenment because religious conservatives dislike the Enlightenment: they consider it too secular. They didn't even get to the parts about Jefferson being now considered more of a Deist (multiple religious authorities) than Christian. But to cut down Jefferson's role, one of the leading Founding Fathers, struck many board members as the Block O' Seven being petty and pedantic, especially since most of the Declaration of Independence for the Republic of Texas was cribbed from Jefferson's work. These folks are revising Texas history books and they don't know this?

More liberal members, not invited to be part of the Block O' Seven, complained about little nagging details like whitewashing the long, hard struggle for civil rights by the minorities in Texas. Some of them are old enough to remember signs on businesses saying, "No Mexicans allowed, no dogs, no Negroes." To leave that out of history books today smacks of Ozzie and Harriet thinking – everyone's happy in their homogenous suburb. That's not even reality on TV anymore.

| *West Texas rain: a sandstorm* |
| --- |

Textbooks get vetted by experts who have a chance to present their concerns to the selection committees, including the Block O' Seven. But the rules say the committees have the final word. This leads to non-experts changing information over the objections of the experts. For instance, McCarthyism is, at least in Texas history books, fully justified by the documents in the Venona Papers outlining communist infiltration into the federal government. And when the experts, world famous historians, said the Venona Papers had been thoroughly discredited? Block O' Seven says, "Too bad, eggheads. What we believe is more important than the facts." (Or something like that – the meetings were closed, another sign something devious is underway).

The punchline to this joke? The budget crisis caused the state to delay purchasing new textbooks in many subject areas. Revisionist history and science is still pending as we write this because the changes won't be made until the budget is approved.

A young male student stomped up to the head librarian at the Texas A&M main library. "I have a complaint," he said.

The head librarian pulled her reading glasses off and let them dangle on the pearl chain around her neck. "I'm sorry to hear that. How may I help you?"

"I got a book here last week, and it was terrible."

The librarian nodded understandingly. "That happens sometimes. What was wrong with it?"

"There were way too many characters, so many I couldn't keep'em straight. But nothing happened in the book. No action, no plot, nothing."

The librarian smiled. "Tell you what, young man. I will pick out a book full of action and plot for you myself, if you do one thing for me."

"Sure, ma'am, what do you want me to do?"

"Bring back our phone book."

When you search for "UT jokes" on Google a few more than 700 results come back and many of those are for the University of Tennessee, not the University of Texas. If you search for "University of Texas jokes" you get about 3,500 results.

If you search for "Texas Aggie jokes" you get over 26,800 results, and nearly 100,000 results if you don't use the quotes when searching. When you search for "aggie jokes" without quotes you get over 637,000 results.

For even more fun, search Amazon for *aggie jokes* and start reading some of the 165 books that appear on your search list. Many are printed by Gigem Press, a company named for the "gig'em Aggie" sports yell.

Yes, an Aggie company printed dozens of Aggie books full of Aggie jokes. But while the rest of us laughed, the Aggie publishing company got our money. And we consider them the dumb ones?

When Sheila, a Maggie (coed from Texas A&M), wanted to lose weight, she was very serious and thorough in her food choices. She ordered a lunch of grilled chicken breast, steamed broccoli with no butter, and a diet water.

Since she was eating at a cafeteria on the Texas A&M campus, they got her diet water from a special bottle without a second thought. They did, however, charge her extra.

## *Go Away, Students*

Students love the University of Texas so much they don't want to graduate. This caused the school some consternation, because while taking more tuition money is easy, building enough more classrooms to keep up with enrollment growth and the six-year graduation plan is hard. The Second Task Force on Enrollment Strategy in early 2010 recommended the school put a ten-semester limit on students.

This won't work, of course, because it's easier to take the tuition money and overcrowd some classrooms. Besides, only about one in fifty students know what they're doing when they start school and don't change their major at least once. And how can you penalize working people taking light loads each semester?

Here's a better idea: make the people who drop out of school, no matter when, leave Austin. Far too many hang around for years and give ne'er do wells a bad name.

On the other hand, name another state university and host

city so nice the school administrators want to drive the students away with a stick.

# Food
# and
# Drink

## *Fresh Donuts & Seafood*

That's the name: Fresh Donuts & Seafood Restaurant in Giddings, Texas (due east from Austin). The address is on East Austin Street (#1510 if you're hungry and looking), but it's really Highway 290 in Central Texas.

They have donuts, and they have seafood and Chinese food. Their blueberry cake donuts are supposed to be wonderful, as are their eggrolls with homemade fish sauce.

## *Order a 150-Pound Texas-Shaped Fruitcake*

Only in Texas, and it's shaped like Texas. Gladys Farek Holub, of Gladys' Bakery in Weimar, Texas, on Highway 10 about halfway between Houston and San Antonio, has retired, but daughter Melissa carries on. Melissa uses the same recipes, because if there's anything you don't want to take a chance on, it's messing up a 150-pound fruitcake.

Gladys and the huge, Texas-shaped fruitcakes have been on both the *Tonight Show with Johnny Carson* and the *Late Show with David Letterman*. And you thought no one cared about fruitcakes anymore.

You can order the Texas shaped cakes as small as 3 pounds, or be bold and go to 5, 10, or 25 pounds. That last step up to 150 pounds will cost you $998.95 (shipping and handling fees apply).

Check them out at gladysfruitcakes.com.

## *Hola, Combination Plate*

When you're in the Dallas area, stop and have a meal at one of the 21 El Fenix restaurants. You'll get a good meal and a big dose of Texas history.

Miguel (Mike) Martinez was born in Mexico but came to Texas in 1911 to avoid the ongoing Mexican Revolution. After marrying Faustina Porras, another Mexican immigrant, and starting on their eight children, Martinez opened a restaurant.

One of the first Texas-Mexican entrepreneurs in Dallas, Martinez served American food at the Martinez Cafe. Since the one-room cafe was in Little Mexico, friends asked for Mexican food. Not too strange a request, so Martinez became one of the first restaurants in Dallas serving Mexican food. But the enchiladas looked a bit odd to the American customers, so Martinez Texan-ized it by pouring some good old Texas chili over the enchiladas. Bingo, the Combination Plate was born. Take an enchilada, tamale, rice, and beans, then pour some chili on top of the enchilada and tamale, and you have a combo plate that has worked for nearly 100 years.

Yo, Yankees, pronounce it tah-mah'-lee, not ta-mail.

Martinez then had all the ingredients, but something was missing. In his case, it tended to be his dishwasher. To cut down on the number of dishes to wash, Martinez put all the food on one large plate rather than the normal method of each item getting its own small plate. Although young kids who don't like their foods to touch each other were unhappy, diners were, and still are, thrilled.

The El Fenix name started in 1922 when Martinez expanded the restaurant. He also made it completely Tex-Mex, the first one ever.

### Is Tex-Mex a Compliment or Insult?

Originally, insult. After all, it wasn't really the Mexican food that people who grew up in Mexico ate. It was different, Anglicized, and bastardized for American tastes. You can't find Tex-Mex in Mexico, except for a few places in heavy tourist areas. But the same is true north of the Red River – finding good Tex-Mex outside of Texas is tough.

On the other hand, Texas is a melting pot of American and Mexican culture and has been for hundreds of years. Taking the best of one culture and adding something from the other is as common a mash-up as a country band playing some Tejano music and vice versa.

Today there are starting to be "real" Mexican restaurants opening in cities around Texas. Not Tex-Mex, but traditional Mexican. That's a good thing. The more each group learns to appreciate the other, the better everyone will get along. Besides, you can't steal the good ideas from another group for your mash-up unless you understand and appreciate them.

## Innovative and Fondly Remembered: Pig Stand

It was 1921, and on Chalk Hill Road in the Oak Cliff section of Dallas, a new restaurant opened. Nothing special about that. But there were two things that made this restaurant unusual. First, the name Pig Stand stood out among the slew of diners around. Second, people could drive their car up to the curb, sit in their car, and get served. Curbside service was born.

Thanks go to Jesse G. Kirby, who noticed that even in 1921, people loved their cars (probably to an unnatural degree, and that continues today). Kirby said that "people with cars are so crazy they don't want to get out of them to eat." People are still that crazy, but at least the cars are much more comfortable now.

When a customer arrived in their Model T at the Pig Stand, a 12 or 13-year-old boy dressed in a white hat, white shirt, and black bow tie would hop on the running board and take the order. When the food was ready, the boy came out and hopped on the running board to deliver the meal. Yep, the invention of carhops.

What is thought to be the first neon restaurant sign ever was on the Pig Stand. A pig outline with the words "Pig Sandwich" in the middle lit the Texas night. That sign and logo stuck with the Pig Stand chain to the very end.

But signs and carhops weren't all that Jesse Kirby created to revolutionize the art of eating out. For people who didn't want to sit in their cars and eat, Pig Stands started offering drive through service. Think of a Pig Stand next time you're driving through McDonalds or Starbucks, or for that matter, any fast food restaurant, or heck, the drive through at your bank. We can't blame Kirby for drive through funeral homes, though. Those are just plain weird.

> *Cook things you can tell what they are. Good plain food ain't committed no crime an' don't need no disguise.*
> *– Mary Lasswell, Honorary Texan, author*

As with many good things we have today, the first onion ring was an accident at, yes, a Pig Stand. A cook dropped a ring of onion aimed toward a hamburger in some batter. He fished it out and, out of habit, flipped the breaded object into the fryer. When browned, the ring of onion with batter on it became the wildly popular onion ring.

Less accidental but just as fun, the Pig Stand in Beaumont wanted their toast to be a bit thicker and more substantial. They asked the local bakery if they could adjust the cutting size of the bread. The bakery did, but with the lack of specific instructions (a "little thicker" means different things to different people, after all), the bread came in too thick for the toaster.

Waste not, want not, so the cook decided to toast the bread the old fashioned way, so he buttered it and threw it on the grill. Shazam! Squared magnificence! Texas Toast was born, and lives on today in restaurants the world over. And you never once thought about a Pig Stand when you ordered either Texas Toast or an onion ring, did you?

A Texas sized piece of toast needed something special, so another Pig Stand culinary genius breaded and fried a piece of tough steak. Probably to hide what looked like a mutant hamburger patty, the cook put it between two pieces of Texas Toast and called it a Chicken Fried Steak Sandwich.

Unfortunately, Pig Stand owners were good at creating and selling the new techniques and food they developed, but really lousy at trademarking them. The Pig Sandwich was protected properly, but not Texas Toast or onion rings or Chicken Fried Steak Sandwiches.

> *You can always tell a Texan, but you can't tell him much.*
> *— The Old Cowboy*

In the 1930s there were over 130 Pig Stands across the country. World War II put an end to any new restaurants, and the number dwindled and dwindled. By 2005 there were a few left around Houston, then, sadly, the company officially went bankrupt.

Today, the only "Pig Stand" left is Mary Ann's Pig Stand in San Antonio. Mary Ann Hill, who started as a Pig Stand waitress at age 18, worked her way up and finally managed one of the last Pig Stand joints in San Antonio. The courts gave Mary Ann the right to build a new Pig Stand from the ground up, not far from the last official restaurant. Mary Ann and several other employees moved from the Pig Stand to Mary Ann's Pig Stand bringing over 225 years of Pig Stand experience behind the aprons.

Restaurants today owe a huge debt to the Pig Stand history of food service innovation. Go to 1508 Broadway in San Antonio and pay homage before it's too late.

### Famous Foods at the Texas State Fair

Fletcher's Corny Dogs may be your favorite guilty Fair food, or maybe the smoked turkey legs. But each year, the State Fair looks for new foods that will go above and beyond calorie counts and fat content. Here's a partial list of recent additions:

- Deep-fried Oreo cookies
- Deep-fried Twinkies
- Deep-fried pork ribs

- Deep-fried cheesecake
- Deep-fried butter (yes, butter)
- Deep-fried peanut butter, jelly, and banana sandwiches
- Deep-fried banana splits
- Deep fried Coke (frozen Coca Cola that's been breaded – they didn't throw a can in the fryer. Maybe next year they'll try that.)

Isn't it strange how all the foods start with "deep fried?" Actually, it may not be a surprise. After all, Fletcher's Corny Dogs are deep fried, and, to double your fun, Corny Dogs are also on a stick.

No less a social leader than Oprah gave her seal of approval to food at the State Fair when she and good buddy Gayle King visited in 2009. But they spent most of their taste buds on winners of the cooking contests, not the fried morsels on the fairgrounds.

For the health and nutrition minded, they should look for deep fried avocados and guacamole. At least under the breading and deep-frying there's a vegetable.

Speaking of contests, fair officials hold one not open to the public: new food ideas from concessionaires. The Big Tex Choice Awards contest started in 2005 (some call it the "stupid people frying stupid stuff" contest). There are two awards: best taste and most creative. Winners not in the list above are, in the creative category:

- Viva Las Vegas Fried Ice Cream
- Deep-Fried Latte

In the best taste category, other winners are:
- Deep-Fried Praline Perfection
- Texas-Fried Cookie Dough
- Fernie's Deep Fried Peaches & Cream

The State Fair, with no fear of contradiction, has been proclaimed the Fried Food Capital of Texas. Long may King of Fried Food reign (that's not applause, that's the sounds of popping and splattering grease and oil). For the non-fried entries, check these out:

- Over the Top Krispy Kreme Donut Burgers (bye bye bun, hello donuts)
- Spaghetti and Meatballs on a Stick.

Oops, the Spaghetti and Meatballs on a Stick is fried. You take cooked spaghetti cut into one-inch length, add meatballs, roll it into a ball, dip it in marinara sauce, roll it in breading, then fry.

One last non-fried option: Kool-Aid Dill Pickles, or Koolickles. Pour out about half the brine from the dill pickle jar and stir in a packet of sweetened Kool-Aid (flavor of your choice). Shake well, and let sit until the pickles start to turn the color of the Kool-Aid flavor, although neon green or red are the favorites. Mmm, red pickles. Appears to be an old southern fair favorite. Wonder why they haven't been deep-fried yet?

Here's a dessert that hasn't been deep-fried: a Cool Dog. In place of the hot dog bun, they use sponge cake. Ice cream replaces the hot dog, and chocolate sauce, whip cream, and sprinkles replace the condiments. Not a drop of frying oil anywhere near the Cool Dog, so you can cool your palate before you try the official State Fair Dessert (at least according to the Texas Hysterical Society).

We proclaim Funnel Cakes the Official State Fair of Texas Dessert. Take light batter, drip it onto the surface of hot oil through a funnel (or cake decorating bag), and fry to almost perfection. Add powdered sugar and serve, and you have the perfect State Fair of Texas dessert. They're small and light, so feel free to have seconds.

## *Big Tex Choice Awards Finalists for 2010*
- Deep-Fried S'mores Pop•Tart®
- Fried Beer™
- Fried Chocolate
- Deep-Fried Frozen Margarita
- Fried Lemonade
- Fernie's Fried Club Salad
- Fried Texas Caviar
- Texas Fried Frito® Pie

Yes, you need to be 21 to order the Fried Beer and Deep Fried Frozen Margarita. The beer is inside a pretzel pocket, and oozes out like a sauce when you bite. The margarita is mixed with Funnel Cake batter and is served in a salt-rimmed glass. Seems a terrible way to treat the wonderful Funnel Cake.

Yes, that's really a club salad including diced ham and chicken, lettuce, carrots, tomatoes, shredded sharp cheddar, and hickory smoked bacon. Take all those ingredients, fold into a huge 12-inch spinach wrap, deep fry, then top with deep fried croutons. Finally, something for those watching their weight. A salad is always healthy, right?

Texas "caviar" is really black-eyed peas with some spices. There are no sturgeons involved (we're not sure if that's good or bad, but there aren't any sturgeons in Texas). You can order your Texas caviar in regular or spicy, but it always comes fried.

Frito Pie, one of the first dishes ungrowed Texans learn to make when they start exploring the kitchen, is a simple recipe. Make some chili (perhaps by opening a can and heating it up), and then pour the chili over a bed of Fritos corn chips. (Fancy meals sometimes include some lettuce to make it more like a taco salad.) Season with shredded cheese to taste. Now take the ingredients, mashed together to hold firm enough to fry, and drop them into the closest fryolator. The contest announcement didn't say if this was going to be on a stick, but this seems like a natural for a handle.

The Fried Lemonade is really more fried lemon flavored pastry, then glazed with a mix of lemonade, lemon zest, and powdered sugar. The Fried Chocolate is a white chocolate mini bar stuffed with a cherry inside a brownies, then deep-fried. Once again, put some powdered sugar on top of the cherry and chocolate sauce.

At this writing, the winner has yet to be announced. But, really, aren't they all winners? And simple, such as deep-frying a Pop-Tart. Of course, for the State Fair of Texas, they plan to add some chocolate syrup and whipped cream to complete the Pop-Tart dish. And, we bet, put it on a stick.

## *Hamburgers Came From Athens, Texas*

Who "created" the hamburger? No, not McDonalds or Burger King. How about Fletcher Davis from Athens, Texas, in the late 1880s? Yep, true.

We can hear the historical fussbudgets starting their whiny engines and saying that the Mongols ground meat into what looked like hamburger, and Russians created Steak Tartar, which is ground steak that looks like hamburger (but at caviar prices, so it ain't no hamburger). And the popular story says Hamburg, Germany, created the hamburger, which is why it has such a funny name. After all, there's no ham in hamburger.

All interesting, but all hogwash. Those examples may be various cuts of meat ground up similar to how we grind hamburger today, but none of those put said meat between two round buns, or even pieces of bread. That honor belongs to Fletcher Davis of Athens, Texas.

In the 1880s, Fletcher "Old Dave" Davis opened a small restaurant and started serving a sandwich that used ground and cooked meat as the filling. People in Athens loved it so much, they convinced Old Dave to schlep up to the 1904 World's Fair in St. Louis and serve it there. No less an authority than

McDonalds says that's where the hamburger started in their official history. No mention of how it got the name hamburger, however.

And for good measure, the Whataburger chain started in Corpus Christi in 1950. Take that, whiny hamburger historical fussbudgets.

## Thomas Munson to the Rescue

Why do the French revere Jerry Lewis, not a Texan, when they should revere T.V. Munson? While Jerry gave us all some laughs (but apparently gave the French many more laughs), Munson saved the French wine industry in the late 1800s, all explained in his book, *Foundations of American Grape Culture*, published in 1909.

An insect cousin of the aphid called the phylloxera loves the grapes used to make wine. While the French were watching the aphid's cousin eat its way through their livelihood (much like some human cousins we know), Munson was busy in Dennison, Texas, making grapevines that didn't taste good to the little phylloxera insects. Think of this as filling the cookie jar with carrot slices, and watching your invading cousins start packing.

The American grape lines used by Munson were carried to France to replenish the vineyards chewed bare by the phylloxera. In fact, Texas grapevines spread across Europe, thanks to Munson.

So the next time you're in a fancy restaurant and the sommelier acts a bit snooty, remind him or her that Texas grapes make fine French wine. When they look surprised, shake your head and say, "It's a shame people don't have the proper respect for Texas history." After all, Munson did receive the French Legion of Honor.

> *We don't eat nothin' that wasn't bigger than we are when it died.*
>
> *— Roland Dickey, restaurateur*
> *In case you ever wondered why Dickey's Barbecue*
> *doesn't serve chicken or turkey, now you know.*

An old cowboy once explained to his son the secret of a long life: sprinkle a little gunpowder on your breakfast each morning. The young man followed those directions and lived to the exalted old age of 97, mentally sharp and healthy to the last.

At the end of his long, happy life, the man left behind 10 children, 33 grandchildren, and 76 great grandchildren. He also left a 15-foot hole in the wall of the crematorium.

## Thank You, San Antonio, for Tex-Mex Food

Visitors may be confused when they learn that Tex-Mex food is really mostly Tex and no Mex. In fact, Mexican foodies strongly object to most famous Tex-Mex dishes. Originally, Tex-Mex was a food insult to non-traditional Mexican food passed off as somewhat Mexican. Now Tex-Mex is a food genre all on its own, and well loved by Texans everywhere (although rarely found north of the Red River).

Harken back to San Antonio at the turn of the century (the other century, 1900), a sleepy little town far away, at least in mental distance, from the capitol Austin. Chicago transplant Otis M. Farnsworth noticed a large number of Anglos liked to eat in small family restaurants in the Mexican part of town. The home-based restaurants were small and a bit south of sanitary, and Farnsworth thought he smelled money along with the chili peppers.

In 1900 Farnsworth started the Original Mexican Restaurant on the San Antonio Riverwalk. He planned on two business advantages: Anglos would prefer to eat closer to home if possible, and the tightening restaurant sanitary standards would cause expensive problems for his mom and pop restaurant competition. By hiring away the best Mexican chefs, and building a modern restaurant with cloth napkins, a professional kitchen, and waiters wearing clean white vests, he could corner the market.

Farnsworth's prognostications turned out to be correct on both counts. The Riverwalk was closer and more familiar to non-Mexican residents, and the health department did tighten up (rumors are at the request of Farnsworth). As the small home-based restaurants closed, Farnsworth did better and better.

For 15 cents (this was 1900, after all), a customer at the Original Mexican Restaurant got a "Regular Mexican Dinner" that included an enchilada with chili gravy, tamales, refried beans, rice, and tortillas. You can get the same dinner, more or less, at every Tex-Mex restaurant in the world today. But if you only leave 15 cents on the table, angry restaurant employees will chase you out into the parking lot and ruin your evening.

# Honorary
# Texans

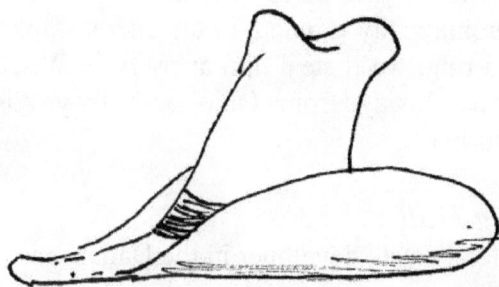

### Sam Houston

Born in Virginia but raised in Tennessee, the two-time President of the Republic of Texas did more than anyone to make Texas, Texas. He is, and always will be, first among Honorary Texans according to the Texas Hysterical Society.

Of course, since there wasn't a Texas when Sam Houston arrived in the area, the Texas Hysterical Society may move at some future time to anoint Houston as First Texan. However, there are so many others who also deserve the rank of being in the group Texas Creators, we'll save that discussion for another book.

### Davy Crockett

You lead a group of men to come give their lives in the Battle of the Alamo to free Texas from Mexican rule, and you become an Honorary Texan of the first rank.

### Larry North

When you make Texans stronger and yourself rich through a chain of personal fitness centers, you get to be an Honorary Texan.

### Roger Staubach

Anyone who helps the Dallas Cowboys win a Super Bowl is automatically granted Texas citizenship. When Tony Romo gets a ring, we'll steal him away from Wisconsin like we stole Staubach away from Ohio and Troy Aikman away from California.

### Craig Hall

Real estate developer in the Dallas area.

### William Cowper Brann

Born in Illinois in 1855, Brann was the owner and editor

of the *Iconoclast* newspaper in Waco from 1895 until his death after being shot in the back in downtown Waco in 1898.

### Shelby Metcalf

Head coach of the Texas A&M basketball team from 1963 until 1990, winning six conference championships in the long gone and long lamented Southwest Conference. He's best known for a razor wit and some wonderful quotes.

### George W. Bush

Two-term Texas governor and two term U.S. President (#43). Born in New Haven, Connecticut, on July 6, 1946, spent formative years in Midland, Odessa, and Connecticut. Any two-term governor of Texas is hereby declared an Honorary Texan.

Those who think George W. Bush (President #43, 2000-2008) is a born Texan, or graduated from college in Texas, have been confused by the hype. Think back and you'll remember he went to Yale, where he was a cheerleader (on the record) and a member of various secret societies like Skull and Bones (conspiracy theories abound). Despite his "good old Texas boy" press image, W only attended one semester of public school in Texas (during middle school).

### George H. W. Bush

Born in Milton, Massachusetts, on June 12, 1924. Moved to West Texas (Midland and Odessa) and got into the oil business, where he struck it rich financially and politically.

### Chuck Norris

Born in Ryan, Oklahoma, Carlos Ray (Chuck) Norris starred in many action films in the 1970s and 80s. His honorary Texan citizenship comes from starring as Cordell Walker in *Walker, Texas Ranger* for 203 episodes from 1993 to 2001. We also appreciate the eight years of Hollywood in North Texas, since all episodes were filmed in and around Dallas and Fort Worth.

### Jerry Jones

Owner of Dallas Cowboys. You bring home three Super Bowl trophies, you are an Honorary Texan, even if you were born in Los Angeles and grew up in Arkansas.

### Kinky Friedman

You name your musical group "Kinky Friedman and the Texas Jewboys" and make waves in the early 1970s in the midst of all the other musical upheavals, and you certainly deserve to the title of Honorary Texan. Run for governor a couple of times, creating more fun quotes than any of a hundred other politicians, and you certainly deserve the title of Honorary Texan. Friedman has done both and more, and is up for the exalted title of Double Honorary Texan.

Born in Chicago on November 1, 1944, Friedman moved to a ranch in Central Texas a few years later to stay close to his parents, Dr. S. Thomas Freidman and Minnie Sarnet Friedman. A chess whiz at an early age, Friedman was one of 50 local players to challenge U.S. Grandmaster Samuel Reshevsky in Houston. How much of a whiz was Kinky? He was seven at the time of the match (he lost).

### Molly Ivins

Born Mary Tyler Ivins in 1944, Molly and family soon moved to Houston, where she grew up to be one of the most quotable Honorary Texans of all time. Her favorite occupation was poking fun at Texas politicians doing stupid things, and she had an endless supply of source material. For some laughs, search on "molly ivins" quotes and prepare to laugh and laugh.

## Edna Gladney

Famous Fort Worth advocate for unwanted children and young unmarried women. Born in Milwaukee in 1886, Edna moved to Fort Worth in 1924 with her husband Sam. By 1927, she was superintendent of the Texas Children's Home and Aid Society. She took over a maternity hospital and renamed it the Edna Gladney Home in 1950. Before her retirement in 1960, she had placed over 10,000 babies with adoptive parents.

## Van Cliburn

His ten talented fingers made a big dent in the wall between the U.S. and Russia during the Cold War when he won the International Tchaikovsky Piano Competition in 1958 at the age of 23. The idea of an American winning was so shocking the judges had to clear their decision with Soviet leader Nikita Khruschev, who, to his credit, said if Cliburn was the best, he deserved the prize. Cliburn was born in Shreveport, Louisiana, but his family brought him to Texas at age six.

## Mary Lasswell

Born in Scotland in 1905, Mary Lasswell grew up in Brownsville, Texas and wrote humorous novels about life in Texas and several lesser places like Southern California, Mexico, and Newark, New Jersey. You may see references to her married name of Mary Lasswell Smith.

# References

*Texas State Historical Association: A Digital Gateway to Texas History.* http://www.tshaonline.org/

Roy R. Barkley and Mark F. Odintz, editors, (2000), *The Portable Handbook of Texas,* Texas State Historical Association.

*The Portable Handbook of Texas*, from the Texas State Historical Association is complete, exhaustive, a bit dry, and heavy. Technically it is portable, but those with weak backs may need to carry it in a wheelbarrow.

Bill Cannon, (1997), *A Treasury of Texas Trivia,* Republic of Texas Press, Lanham, MD.

*101 Aggie Jokes, Volume 7,* (1977) Gigem Press, Dallas, TX.

Jacob Weisberg, (2004), *Bushisms: The Deluxe Post Election Edition,* Fireside, New York, NY.

Susie Kelly Flatau and Lou Halsell Rodenberger (compiled by), (2005), *Quotable Texas Women,* State House Press, Abilene, TX.

*The Story of Texas,* (1986), Shearer Publishing, Fredericksburg, TX.

John Kelso, *Texas Curiosities, Third Edition*, Morris Book Publishing, Guilford, CN.

Sherrie S. McLeRoy, (1997), (2007), *First in the Lone Star*

*State,* Republic of Texas Press, Plano, TX.

Dr. Criswell Freeman, (1995), *The Book of Texas Wisdom,* Walnut Grove Press, Nashville TN.

Steven A. Jent, (2001), *A Browser's Book of Texas Quatiations,* Republic of Texas Press, Plano, TX.

Winter Prosapio and Lisa Wojna, (2007), *Bathroom Book of Texas Trivia,* Blue Bike Books, Alberta, Canada.

Ed Wallace, (2005 and 2008), *The Backside of American History, Volumes I and II,* InsideAutomotive.com

Wallace O. Chariton, (1990), *Texas Wit & Wisdom,* Wordware Publishing, Inc.